Journal

of the

Afro-American Historical & Genealogical Society

2020

VOLUME 37

Journal of the Afro-American Historical and Genealogical Society
P.O. Box 73067, Washington, D.C. 20056-3067
Promoting African American Family Research, Genealogy, and History

Volume 37   ISSN 0271-1937

The *Journal of the Afro-American Historical and Genealogical Society* is an annual publication of the Afro-American Historical and Genealogical Society, Inc. The journal provides a medium for the publication of scholarly essays, and original research on African-American history and genealogy including Africa and Africans in the New World.

Copyright 2019 Afro-American Historical and Genealogical Society, Inc. All material appearing in the journal is copyrighted in the name of the society and is used for the protection of original material published herein, and is not intended to interfere with copyright held by the author.

AAHGS MISSION STATEMENT

The Afro-American Historical and Genealogical Society, Inc. (AAHGS) strives to preserve African-ancestored family history, genealogy, and cultural diversity by teaching research techniques and disseminating information throughout the community. Our primary goals are to promote scholarly research, provide resources for historical and genealogical studies, create a network of persons with similar interests, and assist members in documenting their histories.

EDITORIAL STAFF

Director of Publications: Paula Whatley Matabane
Journal Editor: Stephanie Powers
Design and Layout: Joan Keyes, Dovetail Publishing Services

EDITORIAL BOARD

William Durant	Natonne Elaine Kemp	LaBrenda Garrett-Nelson
Elaine Edwards	Renate Sanders	Guy Oriedo Weston
Sandra El-Amin	Frazine K. Taylor	Robert A. Bellinger

DISCLAIMER

The society does not assume responsibility for errors of fact or interpretation.

EXECUTIVE BOARD 2020

President, Gene Stephenson	*Chapter Committee,* Nathania Branch Miles
Vice President–Genealogy, Vacant	*Membership Coordinator,* Vacant
Vice President–History, Ric Murphy	*Director of Public Relations,* Toni Byrd-Vann
Corresponding Secretary, Alison Barnes	*Librarian/Archivist,* Vacant
Financial Secretary, Vacant	*President Emerita,* Barbara Dodson Walker
Recording Secretary, Stella Pierce	*Immediate Past President,* Sherri Camp
Treasurer, Carolyn Rowe	*Awards Chair,* Jane Taylor Thomas
Director of Publications, Paula Whatley Matabane	*FGS Delegates,* Robert Burch
AAHGS News Editor, Paula Whatley Matabane	*At Large Members Chair,* Robert Wimberly
AAHGS Journal Editor, Stephanie Powers	*Special Projectds,* Marilyn Campbell

ORGANIZATION MEMBERSHIP

AAHGS membership is based on the calendar year. All memberships expire December 31st of each year. Members receive access to online copies of the annual *AAHGS Journal, AAHGS News,* and other benefits offered via the organization website www.AAHGS.org.

AAHGS Membership Types and Rates

Individual $35.00	Organization $45.00
Family $40.00	Lifetime $1,000.00

Submission Guidelines for Contributors

POLICY: The *Journal of the Afro-American Historical and Genealogical Society* (ISSN 0272-1937) is an annual publication of the Afro-American Historical and Genealogical Society, Inc. (AAHGS). Manuscripts are considered for publication if they are not under review elsewhere. All articles and manuscripts submitted for publication are evaluated for appropriateness, validity, and significance and will be edited for clarity, style, and grammar by members of our Editorial Board and persons knowledgeable in the field. The Journal Editorial Board reserves the right to reject manuscripts that do not reflect the mission of AAHGS.

Parts of previously published materials such as maps, photographs, and or illustrations cannot be used without written permission of the author and or copyright holder. Written verification granting permission to use copyrighted material must accompany the manuscript when it is submitted. AAHGS does not assume responsibility for errors of fact or misrepresentation made by our contributors.

GENERAL GUIDELINES: Manuscripts submitted for consideration should conform to one of the following formats:

The Chicago Manual of Style: For Authors, Editors, and Copyrighters (17th Edition, Chicago: University of Chicago Press, 2017,) especially chapters on bibliographic and endnote formats.

Evidence! Citation & Analysis for the Family Historian by Elizabeth Shown Mills (3rd Edition, Baltimore: Genealogical Publishing Co., 2015,) especially chapters on genealogy source citation formats.

The *AAHGS Journal* Style Guidelines. The style guidelines include punctuation, capitalization, terminology, and other preferences specifically adopted by the *AAHGS Journal*.

MANUSCRIPT FORMAT: All information sources must be fully documented with endnotes (not footnotes). Avoid abbreviations.

Manuscript submissions must be double-spaced with one-inch margins on the left, right, top, and bottom. Text must be 12-point size in Times New Roman font. Number the pages. Each manuscript must be no more than twenty pages unless otherwise approved by editor. Writing must be succinct. Overly verbose text will be interpreted as an attempt to unnecessarily increase the page count and will be returned for rewriting.

Author Cover Page: Each author must submit a cover page that includes: the title of article; name(s) of author(s); email address; telephone number; and a brief biography of 70 words or less.

Abstract: Each article must begin with a summary of the larger work. It may contain the thesis, background, problems conducting research and conclusion of the article. The summary must be a self-contained original statement, not an excerpt of the article. The abstract must be 150 words or less.

Tables: Statistical articles (e.g., census enumeration transcriptions, abstracts of tax lists, etc.) must be accompanied by a statement (500 or more words) explaining the historical, social, or economic causes or implications and significance of the data presented or analyzed. Submit tables on separate pages numbered with roman numerals. Each table must be cited in the manuscript text indicating where in the table it should be placed.

Pictures and Graphics: Digital photographs must be submitted in TIFF or high-resolution JPG format at 300 dpi. Camera-ready copies of photographs and graphics must be submitted as separate files from the manuscript. Submit captions for each photo or graphic and indicate suggested locations in the manuscript text.

JOURNAL PUBLICATION PROCESS: Each submission will be reviewed by two members of the journal editorial board whenever possible. Electronic copies of manuscripts must be submitted to journal@aahgs.org.

It is our policy to notify authors of the status of their submissions within six weeks of receipt. Authors may feel free to inquire and send in additional materials (if needed) before the review process is complete. Submitters will be notified as soon as possible if their submissions to meet the criteria, purposes, or focus of this journal and AAHGS.

All persons are welcome and invited to submit to the *Journal of the Afro-American Historical and Genealogical*

Society regardless of race, nationality, age, or academic background including academicians, independent researchers, writers, family historians, genealogists, and students.

MATERIAL ACCEPTABLE FOR PUBLICATION: The *AAHGS Journal* will consider the following types of material for publication:

Manuscripts and articles: Research may focus on government bodies and divisions, organizations, individuals, schools, etc. Scholarly papers presented at meetings, conferences, and workshops but not previously published or under review for publication elsewhere are welcomed.

African and Caribbean history and genealogy: political, legal, and individual histories, slave trade, colonial rule, African literature, traditional cultural practices, resources and methods of research in Africa and Caribbean, etc.

African American history from colonial period to the present: legal issues, political movements, civil rights, traditional cultural practices, African cultural influences or imprints, segregation era, Reconstruction and post-reconstruction, black migrations, free African Americans, etc.

Scholarly papers presented at meetings, conferences, and workshops but not previously published or under review for publication elsewhere are welcomed.

Family histories: family genealogies and biographies, or personal family papers are appropriate. Family histories must have an explanation of significance.

Transcriptions, enumerations, and abstracts: records from federal and city censuses, government departments and statistics, courts, military, labor groups, antebellum plantations, churches, newspaper abstracts, school and community histories, architectural studies, agricultural statistics, etc. are appropriate. Presentation must have an explanation of significance.

Table of Contents

Editor's Note	7
Tony Bowser's Progeny: The Struggle of a Free African American Family, 1676–1860 Benjamin P. Bowser, PhD	9
The Cumbo Family: Tracing one of the First African Descended Families in America Luke Alexander and Andre Kearns	27
City of Renaissance: Frederick Douglass's Baltimore Donna Tyler Hollie, PhD	35
Roots: Tracing the Family History of James McCune and Malvina Barnett Smith, 1783–1937, Part 1 Amy Cools	43
Roots: Tracing the Family History of James McCune and Malvina Barnett Smith, 1783–1937, Part 2 Amy Cools	53
Roots: Tracing the Family History of James McCune and Malvina Barnett Smith, 1783–1937, Part 3 Amy Cools	63
Index	80

Editor's Note

African American history and genealogy are complex. Black lives carry extra implications. The 2020 *AAHGS Journal* reveals multiple implications in different ways.

The authors of *The Cumbo Family* proved they descend from some of the first Africans living in the English American colonies. Their research named enslaved ancestors, bestowing long denied humanity and establishing lineage.

Tony Bowser's *Progeny* documents the perseverance of a "free" African American family despite their fragile legal status governed by the infancy of systematic racism.

City of Renaissance: The Frederick Douglass's Baltimore explores environment versus heredity as the author details the activist's life in Baltimore, Maryland, versus his sister's experiences. The nuanced perspective highlight's the city's unique social climate and Douglass's impact.

The *Family History of James McCune and Malvina Barnett Smith* analyzes the first African American physician's roots. The author reveals how Dr. McCune's upbringing allowed him to treat his people's medical needs while fighting for their civil rights.

Collectively Black people fight for our identity, struggle to retain our freedom, thrive under nurturing circumstances, and force the world to change.

Stephanie Powers
AAHGS Journal editor

Tony Bowser's Progeny: The Struggle of a Free African American Family, 1676–1860

Benjamin P. Bowser, PhD, California State University East Bay

Introduction

My father claimed that his people were "freed Negroes." My mother and I did not believe him. In Harlem of the 1950s, some African Americans claimed they were East Indian, Egyptian, Native American, and all sorts of ancestries, anything but descendants of enslaved Africans. He also commented that as a child, his African American neighbors were named Bowser as well, but, mysteriously, they were not relatives. I never got direct answers to these mysteries because my parents divorced and I wanted no parts of him.

His hometown was Jarvisburg, North Carolina, in Currituck County, near the outer banks of the Atlantic. The first time I visited Jarvisburg was at his funeral in 1986; he passed at 81. I met other Bowsers for the first time; half of the graves in the Corinth Baptist Church cemetery were of Bowsers, unknown to me. After this visit, curiosity got the best of me. I spent hours on microfilm readers searching censuses of Currituck County and was able to do a family tree back to the 1870 census. However, the 1850 and 1860 census slave schedules had no slave owner named Bowser in Currituck County, nor were there any White Bowsers with or without slaves in North Carolina or nearby Virginia in any earlier decennial years—1790 to 1860.

A grave in the cemetery broke the impasse; it was of a Capt. Benjamin Bowser; oddly, it had an American flag flying over it from a ship's mast. In 1994, my sister and I returned to the Corinth Baptist Church for a US Coast Guard ceremony honoring Capt. Benjamin Bowser. He was the second commander of the Pea Island Rescue Station, entirely manned by African Americans after the Civil War; they had an extraordinary record of rescuing passengers and crews of ships that ran aground off the North Carolina coast.

My father never spoke a word about Capt. Bowser. So, I have no idea if he knew about him and if he named me after him. At the ceremony, a local historian greeted me. "We knew there was a scholar named Benjamin Bowser. We wonder when you would show up." I told her that I could not find Bowsers in the 1850 or 1860 census slave schedules. She informed me that the Bowsers were free, and could be found in the regular census (with White people). Then, I was able to trace the family back to Amos Bowser, born in Currituck County in 1823. My father was correct, after all.

The trail went cold again for relatives before 1823; there seemed to be no Bowsers before Amos Bowser in Currituck or surrounding counties. My local historian provided a second key. Freed African Americans in Currituck County fled nearby Virginia around 1800. To my surprise, Bowsers before the first census (1790) were in Paul Heinegg's *Free African Americans of Virginia, North Carolina, South Carolina, Maryland and Delaware* (2009). The earliest Bowser was Anthony Bowser in Virginia.

> "Anthony Bowser, born say 1650, was called '**Tony Bowze Negro late Servt to Major Genn**' Bennett Deceased" when he petitioned the Virginia General Court in March 1676 for his freedom which was granted on his payment of 800 pounds of tobacco yearly" [McIlwaine, Minutes of the Council and General Court of Colonial Virginia, 1622–1632, 1670–1676, 437] (Heinegg 2005).

Heinegg found approximately 70 other Bowsers in the Virginia colonial records from 1700 through 1806 who were presumably the progeny of Anthony Bowser. It took a while to realize the implications of these findings. First, it was very likely that Jonas Bowser, born in nearby Currituck County in 1823, was related to Anthony Bowser. Second, my known lineage may go back from the year 2019, not 149 years to the Civil War, not 241 years to the Revolutionary War, but 369 years, just one generation after the 1619 first sale of 20 enslaved Africans at Jamestown, Virginia. Third, my grandfather did not know their family connection with his African American neighbors, also named Bowser. By 1920 when my father was a teen, this knowledge could have been lost easily with a lineage going back over 270 years. Finally, Bowsers had remained free from the beginning of slavery in British North America and the hostility of Whites toward African descendants in Virginia and North Carolina for eight generations until 1863. An essential question arose. How was Anthony Bowser's progeny able to survive, physically and psychologically, as freed people for so long? What did they experience? This paper uses a genealogical search to explore this historical question.

Anthony Bowser

Who was Major General Richard Bennett, Anthony Bowser's master? He was baptized in 1609, died in 1675, and was from one of the earliest Virginia settlers (Fausz 2015). His uncle and brother came to North America because of Virginia's economic promise and because of their extensive international trade experience and contacts. After their deaths, Richard took over their affairs and successfully amassed more than 7,000 acres of land in Virginia and Maryland and 1,300 slaves to grow tobacco. He became the wealthiest man in Virginia, served twice on the Virginia governor's council (1642–1652; 1658–1675) and as governor (1652–1655). The political and economic success of the Virginia and Maryland colonies was mainly due to his political leadership. In his will, he left 1,000 pounds of tobacco at his death to each of his servants (Principle Probate Registry 1960). It is from this gift that Anthony Bowser paid for his freedom from indentured service the year after Bennett died.

Who was Anthony Bowser? How did this African descendant get to Virginia and into Richard Bennett's service? If he was an enslaved African and sold to someone named Bowser, his master's name should appear among the earliest Virginians and perhaps Marylanders as well. It does not. None of the initial Jamestown settlers was named Bowser, nor was there a Bowser on any of the ships' manifests of settlers who landed in Virginia between 1609 and 1650. There was no Bowser among the earliest Huguenots. There was no Jamestown settler with a name even close in spelling to Bowser. Bowser, with this exact spelling, is an old English family surname, common in Yorkshire. It dates back to medieval times with French Norman roots as "Bousser" (Wagner 1966). The first English Bowser to land in Virginia was named "Hen Bowser." She arrived without family in 1666 (Ancestry.com 2010)—too late to have been Anthony Bowser's master.

There is a key to Anthony Bowser's origin as well as to his name. In the early 1600s, the largest concentration of Englishmen in North America was on Barbados, Great Britain's North American colonial headquarters. In 1638, an Englishman named Anthony Bowser was a Barbadian plantation owner with more than ten acres of land (Arnold 1884). He was the only plantation owner on Barbados named Bowser. Perhaps, this Englishman bought an enslaved African who had a son sometime around 1650. They named the enslaved son, Anthony Bowser, after the master. By the 1673 census of Barbadian plantation owners, no Bowser was listed, nor was any Bowser listed as an island resident in later censuses (Governor of Barbados 1979; Atkins 1988). About this time, small Barbadian plantation owners were brought out to make way for more extensive and more profitable sugar plantations (Stuart 2013). Familysearch.org identified 69 Anthony Bowsers in England between 1600 and 1700. Only three were in the age range of the Barbadian slave owner,

Anthony Bowser. The first died 26 April 1663; the second was married on 29 January 1658 to an Elizabeth Clifford; and the third was buried in 1643 in Bristol, Gloucester. Any one of these men could have been the master of the enslaved father and son.

Before the Englishman Anthony Bowser returned to England (or otherwise disappeared), Richard Bennett brought the African descendant Anthony Bowser. It was no minor feat to become a household servant of the richest man in Virginia. Bennett already had access to slaves in Virginia and Maryland. Perhaps, Anthony Bowser was trained to serve a man of Richard Bennett's high standing by his father and owner. It is significant that when Anthony Bowser petitioned for his freedom, he was identified as a servant, not a slave. In 1676, slavery in Virginia was still evolving into a distinct institution from English indentured servitude. Thus, servitude and slavery were confounded until the Virginia planter elite decided that enslaved Africans were less dangerous to them than an exploited servant class (Morgan 1975, 308). In whatever way it happened, the servant Anthony Bowser was positioned well to benefit from his freedom after 1676. He had skills as a household servant; he may have been literate, and, undoubtedly, he knew the wealth friends and family of the deceased former governor. However, Bacon's Rebellion happened the very year Anthony Bowser received his freedom, and, after that, opportunities of free African Americans to advance socially and economically were sharply curtailed (Green and Innes 2005, xiii). What happened to Anthony Bowser's progeny? The answer to this question requires laying out the contexts and constraints that Bowsers and other free African Americans, identified by Paul Heinegg, most likely lived under during the 1700s.

Methods

First, Bowser turns out to be an ideal name to do genealogy research in colonial Virginia. English (White) Bowsers did not immigrate to North America until 1774 (Bowser 1922). When they did, they first settled in Pennsylvania. Therefore, all the colonial Virginia and North Carolina Bowsers before 1774 were very likely the progeny of Anthony Bowser. Paul Heinegg identified approximately 70 Bowsers in Virginia colonial records through 1806.

Bowsers found by Heinegg did not represent all of Anthony Bowser's progeny. However, those found tell us something about their collective experiences and that of other free African Americans like them. Methodologically, our task is to make inferences from the Heinegg findings to derive insights about the lives of free African Americans. Sociologists and other social scientists presume that with enough contextual details, one can approximate lived experiences in the past and present.

Furthermore, along with a comparative approach, contextual details can be juxta-positioned with one another to reveal additional insights. Three contexts, drawn from the early Virginia Chesapeake Bay region, will be used to made inferences about Bowsers and other free African Americans from 1700 to 1860. There are many other contextual variables (Earle 1975). However, the most important contexts for Free African Americans are the the economy, community, and legal-racial. The economic and community contexts come from extensive research done on the Chesapeake eighteenth-century tidewater and piedmont counties (Kulikoff 1986; Earle 1975). The legal-racial context is intrinsic to the history of free African Americans. Finally, the Chesapeake regional trends adopted in this paper are not unique to the Chesapeake. They apply to other plantation agricultural counties in the 1700s (Earle 1975; Megginson 2006). With the three contextual factors, one can analyze the colonial records of free African American Bowsers and others.

Anthony Bowser's Children: 1700s
Economic Context

The capacity to form and sustain a family is dependent upon one's ability to support them materially. The counties that make up the Virginia Chesapeake Bay regional economy in the 1700s divided into two areas, the tidewater, and piedmont (Kulikoff 1986). In the tidewater, land along rivers and the seacoast were the earliest settled, farmed, and developed economically, beginning with Jamestown in 1609. The same developmental pattern was noted for All Hallow's Parish, Maryland (Earle 1975). By 1750, subsistent farming and free labor had given way to large tobacco plantations and slave labor. Land values increased as did taxes. Land and slaves were the keys to higher status and comfort; the more of each, the wealthier one became (Wright 1978, 37). Captured Africans were imported as slaves after 1660 at such a rate that the slave population doubled every decade (Kulikoff 1986, 65). Their rate of growth far exceeded that for Whites. As slaves became more numerous and skilled, there was less work for free White and Black labor alike. Thus, free laborers found it increasingly difficult to buy land to advance economically in the tidewater. By 1750, available land in the tidewater disappeared, and an out-migration of free labor to the piedmont had been going on for some time. Landless laborers were forced to move further west into the interior of Virginia away from the coastal tidewaters.

In the piedmont, the land was cheaper; taxes were lower than in the tidewater. There were few plantations and slaves. However, it was challenging to bring tobacco or any other produce to markets because roads were nonexistent, few were passable, and upcountry rivers were not navigable. Also, from 1680 to 1715, the price of tobacco declined, and exports stagnated, depressing the economy and opportunities for work in both the tidewater and piedmont. In response, from 1700 to 1740, planters grew even more tobacco to offset their losses. Increasing tobacco required importing even more African slaves, further reducing work for free labor (Kulikoff 1986, 65; Earle 1975). Those who had to sell their labor to survive had to choose between two bad options—the tidewater or the piedmont—as opportunities for work disappeared. Most failed in their quest to buy land and gain wealth wherever they settled (Kulikoff 1986, 152). From the beginning, Bowser progeny were in trouble.

By 1790, the entire tobacco economy collapses; farmers and large planters alike had to transition to less profitable general farming (Kulikoff 1986, 157). Also, piedmont lands to settle on disappeared. At the same time, the American Revolutionary War produced a flood of Quaker and Baptist inspired manumissions of African slaves (Kolchin 1993), creating "a substantial class of free black people in the (Chesapeake) region for the first time" (Kulikoff 1986, 419). The timing of these manumissions could not have been worse. New and longtime free African Americans fell to the absolute bottom of the labor force; many found themselves out of the economy altogether. The fortunate ones found whatever remaining work as agricultural laborers and sharecroppers.

Community Context

Community development in the Chesapeake region followed the economy closely, and there were stages in its formation across several generations. In stage one, Indians were driven from their land, squatters came, cleared the land, and began subsistent farming. In stage two, speculators followed, claimed as much land as possible, and drove squatters away. Aspiring settlers followed to claim the remaining land or to buy small plots from speculators. Clearing and working newly opened land was extremely dangerous and laborious. Settlers had to work their plots until there were enough of them to assist one another. In stage three, practical interdependencies led to "informal groupings of neighbors, men, women, church members, and kin" (Kulikoff 1986, 206). In stage four, neighboring children intermarried, and their families formed clans and extended families. By this point, community life organized increasingly around kin rather than unrelated neighbors. Those most similar in status, wealth and religion associated increasingly with one another. In the final stage, there were sufficient numbers and social organization among residents to open and support stores, taverns, and other businesses to form towns. Anglican churches were the first neighborhood institution. They required all adults to attend service monthly and report members' births, marriages, and deaths.

Legal-Racial Context

Freed African-Americans were citizens with the same rights as Whites. Instead, the colonial Virginia legislature passed laws specifically against free African Americans. A 1705 law made free African American and non-reservation Indian wives over 16 years old subject to an individual tax. Free African Americans were denied the right to vote in 1723; they were prohibited from testifying against Whites after 1732 and were entirely denied citizenship in 1779. A 1793 law required free African Americans to register with their town or county clerk and to carry their registration papers at all times (Bogger 1997, 25). In 1806, the most drastic law was passed after the 1800 Gabriel Conspiracy (Crow 1977, 88). Any newly manumitted African Americans had to leave the state within a year, and any African Americans already free who left the State could not return. The penalty for violating any of these laws was to be tried and, if convicted, returned into slavery.

Bowsers in Early Virginia

Economy: The Heinegg records give us clues to what Bowsers experienced in Virginia's Nansemond, Southampton, and the Isle of Wight Counties (Heinegg 2005). The Bowsers identified by Paul Heinegg in the Virginia colonial records did not own property, the key to comfort and wealth. There were no records found of Bowser land purchased or sells. If any Bowsers owned land, there would have been tax records. A few paid taxes on farm animals and items indicating that they were tenant farmers—sharecroppers. By inference, identified and unidentified Bowsers must have been poor; people who did not show up on tax records had nothing of taxable value. To survive materially and remain in the three counties, they had only two ways to survive—wage labor and sharecropping.

Community: In the settler to interdependent stages (2–3), free African Americans were more likely accepted as neighbors. However, once clans and social hierarchies formed (stages 4–5), there was closure around family, social class, and church membership. By this point, it was less likely that free African Americans were accepted as new residents or had continuing acceptance as long-term residents. Bowser families were scattered across Virginia's Nansemond, Southampton, and Isle of Wright Counties. Their early start in these counties with Anthony Bowser's freedom in 1676 put them at stages 2–3 in county development. They likely found acceptance as early residents. However, as these counties developed beyond stage three sometime after 1750, their and other free African Americans' presence became increasingly problematic in the broader community if not for their immediate White neighbors.

Laws: There is a view among students of free African Americans in colonial Virginia and North Carolina that laws against them were rarely enforced and were, therefore, ineffective (Franklin 1971, 58, 195). Plus, these laws were enforced sporadically. Such an assessment misses the effect of these laws beyond the courts. Anti-free African Americans laws did not have to be enforced to do damage. For free African Americans to know of such laws and the ongoing potential of persecution against them, enforced or not, had to be a source of insecurity and a psychological burden.

Anti-free African America laws were intended to make it difficult for them to survive, prosper, and remain in Virginia. The laws signaled to Whites that free Blacks did not have rights that Whites had to respect, and they could be abused with impunity. Anti-free Black laws made it possible for a White person to claim at any time that a free African American was, in fact, a runaway slave. Then, they could be jailed and not allowed to testify on their behalf. Once accused, the only acceptable proof of free-status was the testimony of a White person, willing to swear that the freed African American person, their parents, and perhaps even their grandparents had lived as free people in the county for generations. Another law required that every Free African American man, woman and child carry papers verifying their status as a free person. How does one carry such papers all the time for one's entire life? Under the circumstance, it was perilous to move to another county where one's history as a free person was unknown or where Whites did not know one well enough to testify on one's behalf. One could be re-enslaved with no recourse.

There was another passive negative effect of the laws against free African Americans. Bowser families remained in Nansemond, Southampton and the Isle of Wight counties even as these counties developed, as opportunities to buy land declined, as their poverty increased, and as hostility increased to their presence. The laws that made them vulnerable to re-enslavement made moving to another county to pursue better opportunities more dangerous and precarious than staying where they were. They had to remain in place to have White neighbors who could vouch for their long-term residence and status as free people.

Paul Heinegg provided three additional factors that add to the economic, community, and legal contexts. These factors tell us more about the lived experiences of Bowser families in Virginia in the 1700s. In the Virginia colonial records, Bowser children were bound out, some Bowsers were tithable (liability for taxes) and, surprisingly, four owned slaves (Heinegg 2005).

Bowsers Bound Out

Heinegg's most frequent finding in the Virginia Colonial records was of Bowser children "bound out." County residents, generally neighbors, could alert local authorities that a family was unable to properly cloth, feed, and care for one or more of their children (Herndon and Murray 2009). The matter was brought before the county court to decide if the parent(s) was, indeed, unable to provide. If parents were not able, the authorities could "bound out" the child (or children). The sheriff, as the agent of the court, would take the child from his or her parent(s) and place them with another family that could adequately care for them. The child lived with this family until he or she reached a certain age—generally 21. During this time, the foster family was committed to teaching the child a trade by which the child could become financially self-sufficient as an adult.

Having children bound out tells us several things. First, it showed that the household was financially impoverished. Second, according to the records, most children bound out were from single female-headed households. Third, bounding out indicated that the male "breadwinner" and father of the children were dead, disabled, worked elsewhere, did not earn enough to support his family, or had abandoned the mother and children. Fourth, if one child among several was bound-out, it suggested abuse or neglect of that particular child or that the family could get by if it had one less child. Fifth, bounding out indicated a failure or inability on the part of the extended family to step in and care for the child or children. If the extended family could not intervene, then a bounding out suggested that the extended family, as well as the immediate parents, might have been impoverished. Finally, bounding out indicated that there was not in the impoverished family's life an extended community of church, neighbors, or friends able to step in and assist the child's parent(s) sufficiently to keep the parents and children together. In effect, bounding-out forewarned of a family's complete breakdown and demise.

The most frequent bounding out of Bowser children appeared in court records in 1778 and 1783. These bounding outs occurred just as manumissions from slavery increased, and as the tobacco economy collapsed. Economically, this was the worst possible time. Three children bound outs in 1778 were Sarah Bowser's, and three others were "orphaned mulatto" Bowsers. There are several additional explanations for the timing of these interventions. Before 1778, the lack of children bound out suggests that Bowser families, while poor, were able to support themselves. Perhaps, earlier in the century, some families had collapsed and disappeared before the county was able to intervene and bound out their children. Perhaps, records were better kept after 1770. Finally, it is possible that bounding out after 1770 was used in some way to discourage or punish free African Americans.

Tithable Bowsers

To be tithable is to be liable for the payment of taxes imposed by the colonial legislature. The second most frequent eighteenth-century Virginia record of Bowsers was their annual county tax liabilities. Counties had a specific list of taxable possessions. Each horse, mare, pig, cow, head of cattle, and living on rental property was taxable. There was also a tax on the number of people in one's household. Again, all of the Bowser tax records appeared after 1770, not before. That some were able to pay taxes meant that not all Bowsers were impoverished. The basis of their ability to pay was most likely for tenant farming since there were no records of their owning land.

Bounding out and tithability suggest that Bowser families in the three counties ranged across the lower economic strata. At one end, they were laborers barely able to provide for their children, and, on the other end, they were tenant farmers. If there were relatively well-off Bowser families, they did not support the families whose children were bound out. Perhaps, family conflicts alienated them from one another. Alternatively, by the end of the century, they may not have thought they were related, despite having the same surname.

Bowser Slaves

There was a surprise in the colonial records. Four Bowser households paid taxes for slaves. The number of slaves owned by each family ranged from one to four. Each household record gave detail about the slaves—their first name, gender, age, and the number of them. There were even different tax rates for slaves over 16 years old, from ages 12 to 16, and younger than 12.

Students of Virginia free African Americans caution that in some cases, these slaves were, in fact, husbands, wives, and children (Franklin 1971, 160). Free African Americans had to buy enslaved relatives to keep their family together and eventually to emancipate them. For example, James Bowser, who served in the Revolutionary War, owned the four slaves. On 5 September 1800, he freed from slavery a "Negro Bridget, aged 57." He stated in his Isle of Wright County deed emancipating her that "freedom is a natural right." On the same day, he made an oral will, apparently while dying, leaving his whole estate to his wife, "Bridget Bowzer." Is it a coincidence that the slave and wife had the same name? The slave "Negro Bridget" was very likely his wife, "Bridget Bowzer." Then, ironically, the widow Bridget Bowzer, now a free African American, was held liable for taxes on 2–3 other slaves for six years afterward.

Fleeing to North Carolina

Bowsers eventually ventured away from Nansemond, Southampton, and Isle of Wight counties. Heinegg's records show that several showed up in North Carolina counties after 1750. A family was in Hertford County in 1768 and 1779; in Warren County in 1780; in Halifax County in 1800; and in Brunswick County, Virginia, by 1826. Each County was further west than its Virginia counties of origin. Perhaps, the attractiveness of opportunities further west along the border of Virginia and North Carolina in new piedmonts outweighed the increasing difficulties of living in Nansemond, Southampton and the Isle of Wight.

In 1784, Cressa, Hamilton, Ella, and Sally Bowser made it very clear that they saw no future in Virginia, North Carolina, or any place else where Whites ruled; they fled to Liberia (Heinegg 2005). Still, others fled first to Currituck County, North Carolina, and, by 1810, to Dorchester, Baltimore, Harford, Maryland, and Philadelphia. Fortunately, through the North Carolina GenWeb Archives, Currituck County court records, deeds, and census files are available from 1790–1866. These records provide an opportunity for a less speculative reconstruction of free African Americans living in antebellum North Carolina. They also provide an opportunity to compare the fate of Bowsers with other Heinegg identified free African Americans who might have also migrated to Currituck County.

Anthony Bowser's Children in North Carolina: 1800 to 1860

In 1800, North Carolina was a new piedmont where there was potential for work, to buy land,

and lives freely that no longer existed in Eastern Virginia. Consequently, free White and Black Virginians had been migrating into North Carolina for land since 1750.

Currituck County

Currituck County is just across the Virginia-North Carolina border nearest Nansemond, Isle of Wright, and Southampton Counties. The county has three physical typographies (see figure 1). The northern districts are first. Moyock, Gibbs Woods, Knotts Island, Tull Creek, and the Currituck Court House consist primarily of flat open land with occasional woods and are indistinguishable from southern Virginia. No geographic feature marks the state border. Traveling south in the County, one passes through Moyock to get to Tull Creek and then Court House. The middle districts of Coinjock, Poplar Branch, and Powells Point are the second typography, which runs south on a progressively narrowing peninsula with North River to the west and Currituck Sound on the east. The further south one goes the closer is water access on the west and east sides. The Outer Banks, a 200-mile long string of barrier islands, parallel the Currituck peninsula to the east and is easily accessible by small boats. The third typography is Roanoke Island, which sits to the south of the Currituck peninsula and is close to the Outer Banks. The second and third typographies have numerous inlets and landings, and ways to hide and escape by water. Roanoke Island once had a small harbor where shallow draft ships accessed the Atlantic until weather and tides permanently closed the harbor's inlet through the Outer Banks.

North Carolina had a reputation as a haven for fugitive slaves (Crow 1977, 40). Currituck County on the North Carolina-Virginia State line is partly responsible for this reputation. Throughout the 1700s, the Outer Banks was a refuge for mulattos fleeing Virginia's 1710 and 1723 laws against mix-racial marriages. Indian refugees from the Tuscarora War and mixed-racial children of Indian and English traders sought refuge on the Outer Banks as well (Cecelski 2001). During the Revolutionary

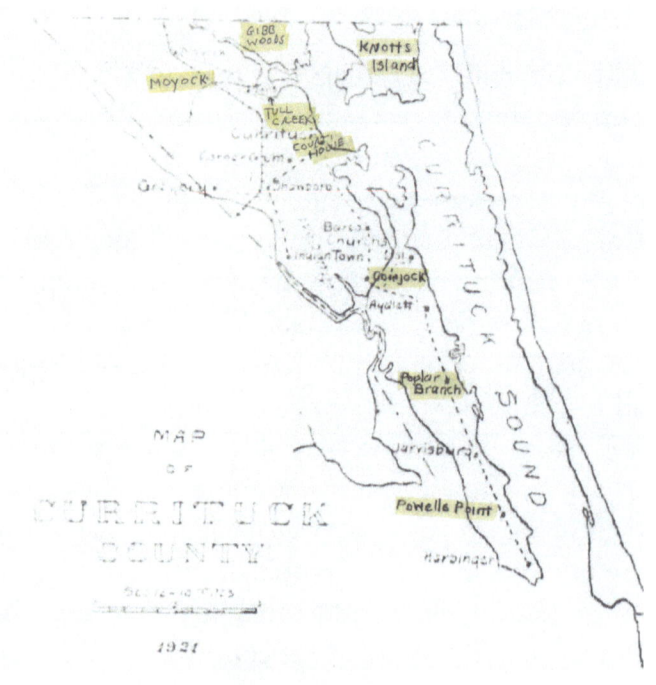

Source: The Independent (Elizabeth City, NC weekly) - Friday, January 6, 1922; pg. 11

Figure 1   Map of Currituck County

War, Currituck County is, reputedly, where slaves planned to flee Virginia to join the British who promised them freedom (Crow 1977, 61); however, Robert Howe blocked their escape. The middle and Roanoke districts of Currituck County were attractive to free African Americans as well because their remoteness and limited space discouraged plantation agriculture (Cecelski 2001, 12). Finally, local fishery owners preferred to employ free African Americans rather than slaves.

The move to North Carolina initially appeared promising. The Currituck County Deed Book identified a James Bowser as a property owner on remote Roanoke Island in 1790 (County 1790). Two of the final Heinegg recorded Bowsers were women heading households in Currituck County—"Rachel head of a Currituck County household of 3 'other free' in 1800," and "Mary (Bowser), born 1780, 70-year-old 'Mulatto' woman counted in the Currituck County census in 1850" (Heinegg 2005). At that time, it was common for husbands and fathers to be absent from their household (Bogger 1997, 109); many were hired as farm laborers and work required them to live away from home. These two settler families very likely lived in the Northern-most part of Currituck nearest Virginia. In 1800, the area between the state border and Court House was still developing, and there were hardly roads further south into the more remote part of the County where James Bowser of Roanoke Island had property. However, there was a place where free African American men in southern Virginia and northern North Carolina were welcomed. It is likely that Bowser men, along with other free African Americans, worked digging canals through the Dismal Swamp, just northwest of Currituck. They were welcome because slaves were too valuable to risk because of the diseases, accidents, injury, and deaths doing such dangerous work (Bogger 1997, 87–88).

Bowsers were not the only free African Americans to flee Virginia for Currituck County for land, work, and to sharecrop. The 1790 Census of Population was the first attempt to enumerate the county's population. It identified 115 free African Americans, whose names were compared with Virginia free African Americans identified by Paul Heinegg. They included Case, Gordon, Gregory, Hunt, Hiter, Patterson, Sanderlin, Spelman, Thomas, and Wilson family members (See Appendix A for a list of Currituck County free African Americans found in each census through 1860). One way to become a tenant farmer in Currituck County was to lease land from Whites and promise to improve it, as did James Spellman. On 10 acres, he promised "to put the high ground under good fencing …" and "to build a three-foot ditch and other ditches sufficient to drain the land . . ." (County 1796, 55–56). What kind of economy did James, Rachel, Mary Bowser, and other free African Americans content with until the Civil War?

Currituck Economic Context

Currituck County's economy in 1800 was an extension of the Virginia piedmont, consisting primarily of small farms. Like Virginia, Currituck began with relatively inexpensive land settled by pioneers who cleared it and begun subsistence farming. Change in the White population was an indicator of economic growth or decline, increasing with economic growth and declining in recessions (Kulikoff 1986, 45). The same dynamic applied to slaves. When owners' wealth increased, they bought more land and slaves; when their wealth decreased, they sold both. Table 1 shows changes in the number of Whites, households, slaves, and free African American populations from 1790 through 1860.

In sixty years, there was modest growth in the number of households (20.7%) as well as in total population (35.9%). The rate of growth in the White population was slightly less than half (16.6%) of the total population's growth. In contrast, between 1790 and 1860, the number of slaves doubled (99.7%), as did the small number of free African Americans (93.9%) in the County. A decline followed the increase in Whites and slaves until 1830. These statistics suggest rapid economic growth and generation of wealth in Currituck County until 1830, followed by modest growth afterward. Generally, where slavery expanded, the free African American population was unwelcomed and declined in size. In this case, both the slave and free populations increased over time.

Several events could account for the fall in the White population and modest economic growth after 1830. The canal system running through the nearby Dismal Swamp enabled Currituck County farmers to ship crops and livestock conveniently into Virginia and to northern markets. However, advances in railroad technology rendered the canal obsolete at its completion; trains could run almost anywhere, eliminating the need for the canal. Then, land in the Western US opened; half the counties in North Carolina, including Currituck, lost population (Cecelski 2001, 117).

Predictably, a decline in slaves by 1840 follows the loss in the White population and agricultural production by 1830. However, afterward, the number of slaves went up faster than did the White population. Thirty-one percent of North Carolina families owned slaves in 1790 (Carbone 2001, 87);

Table 1 Racial Demographics, Currituck County, NC, 1790–1860 Censuses

Year	1790	1800	1830	1840	1850	1860	Percent Growth
Total Population	5219	5617	7654	6677	7265	7095	35.9
White Population	4001	3403	5334	4430	4582	4665	16.6
Households	792	1072	1095	892	926	956	20.7
Slaves	1103	1667	2188	2099	2484	2203	99.7
Free Blacks	115		132	148	192	223	93.9

Source: U.S. Bureau of the Census, Census of Population, Currituck County, North Carolina, 1790-1860; U.S. Bureau of the Census, Slave Schedule, Currituck County, North Carolina, 1850–1860.

Table 2

	Total Whites	Total White Slave Owner	% Whites Who Own Slaves	Slave Min	Slaves Max (Owner)	Average Slaves Per Owner
1790	4001	256	6.4	1	23 (John Humphries)	4.3
1800	3403	387	11.4	1	26 (Joseph Gray)	3.9
1830	5334	396	7.4	1	43 (Daniel Lindsey, Jr.)	5.5
1840	4430	349	7.9	1	31 (Samuel Ferebee)	6.0
1850	4582	205	4.4	1	43 (Hodges Gallop)	7.0
1860	4665	243	5.2	1	91 (G.C. Marchant)	8.4

Source: U.S. Bureau of the Census, Census of Population, Currituck County, North Carolina, 1790–1860; U.S. Bureau of the Census, Slave Schedule, Currituck County, North Carolina, 1850-1860.

Table 3 Average Value of Land and Personal Property by Slave Ownership, Currituck County, 1850 and 1860

	1850 Value Land	Number Residents	1860 Value Land	Number Residents	1860 Value Property	Number Residents
Do Not Own Slaves	$ 741	406	$ 1,060	434	$ 1,336	434
Own Slaves	$ 1,333	144	$ 6,319	204	$ 5,986	204
Total	$ 896	550	$ 2,742	638	$ 2,823	638
	$F = 15.2; p < .000$		$F = 9.7; p < .002$		$F = 94; p < .000$	

Source: U.S. Bureau of the Census, Census of Population, Currituck County, North Carolina, 1790–1860; U.S. Bureau of the Census, Slave Schedule, Currituck County, North Carolina, 1850–1860.

67 percent of slaveholding families had fewer than ten slaves by 1860. Seventy-two percent of North Carolina families held no slaves at all (Franklin 1971, 147). Currituck County was right in line with the State of North Carolina in terms of growth in the White population and slaves. What follows are the total White population, number of Whites who owned slaves, the percentage of Whites with slaves, and the minimum and maximum number of slaves. The average number of slaves owned by White owners from 1790 to 1860 follows the family name of the largest owner at each decennial year.

In table two, the highest percentage of Currituck County Whites to own slaves was 11.4 percent in 1800; the lowest percent was 4.4 percent in 1850. See Appendix B for the names of the top five slave owners for each decennial year. Table two tells us a great deal about work and slavery in the County. The vast majority of White county residents were small farmers who did not own slaves. Slave owners had, on average, 4.3 slaves in 1790 and 8.4 slaves by 1860, a steady increase.

The Virginia tidewater-piedmont experience was that the more land and slaves a slaveholder had, the more money they could make—that was the purpose of slavery. Was this the case for Currituck County? The 1850 census recorded the value of one's land, and the 1860 census asked the value of one's land and personal property. From responses to these questions, the better-off-with-land-and-slaves assumption was tested. The results follow:

Census respondents in both 1850 and 1860 confirmed the better-off-with-slaves-and-land assumption. In 1850, non-slaveholders reported significantly lower average land value (average $741) than slaveholders (average $1333). In 1860, non-slaveholders reported significantly less average land value (average $1060) and less average property value ($1336) than slaveholders' land (average $6319) and property (average $5986). The five-fold increase in the value of slave-owner property between 1850 and 1860 was observed as well in other parts of the South (Wright 1978, 35). In Currituck County, this jump in wealth may be due to several owners who significantly increased their landholdings and smaller landholders abandoning the County. If anything, these self-reported values were under-estimated in each decennial year. Owners reported lower values to avoid paying higher taxes.

Currituck County defies convention in another way. Slave owners were suspicious of free African Americans whose contact with their slaves could make them rebellious and aspire to freedom. Therefore, they did not want free African Americans living near their farms and plantations (Franklin 1971, 196; Jackson 1971, 91). A close look at the censuses for Currituck County reveals a more complex picture. Of course, there were landowners with only slaves as labor. However, there was a small group of White landowners in each decennial year who employed only free African Americans as laborers; they had no slaves as laborers. Then, there were landowners with both slaves and free Blacks as laborers, mixing the two. The same observation was made of slave-landholders in the South Carolina piedmont (Megginson 2006, 29). Furthermore, the number of slaves owned by Whites with no free Blacks in their household was not significantly different from the number of slaves in households with free Black labor (analysis not shown). Slave labor for small planters was not essential to financial success; one could use slaves, free labor or a combination of both.

The above findings suggest that one way free African Americans were able to survive financially in Currituck County was through farm labor in White households who may or may not have had slaves. This fact suggests that the cost of their labor to white farmers may not have been very different from the cost of slave labor. An estimated of Chesapeake tobacco farming in 1830 is that the cost of slave labor was $51 per year per slave, half was one's purchase cost averaged over 30 years (Earle 1978). The cost of free labor was $95 per year per person, split between wages and maintenance. However, to get this low cost for slave labor requires high startup down payments or access to credit. Young, healthy slaves in 1830 could cost as much as $800–$900 each. Currituck County Deed books showed that the cost of slaves ranged dependent on their gender, age, and health. In 1789, a Negro woman sold for £300 ($375), and a 16-year-old girl sold for £950 ($1,217). In 1812, a 40-year-old Negro woman sold for £170 ($212). By 1841, a Negro boy sold for $690.

Most Currituck small farmers had neither large down payments nor access to credit to buy slaves. Credit and initial startup capital are precisely what separated elite Virginia Chesapeake planters from all other farmers (Morgan 1975, 304–5). Also, wheat, corn, and other non-tobacco corps did not need year-round labor. If a farmer pays for no more than five months of work, free labor-costs drop to $40 per year per person. Then, if they cut the cost of maintenance in half ($20 to $10) and pay free Black labor less than White labor, farm labor costs could drop below $30 per worker per year. This cost is considerably less cost for labor ($30 versus $51) and does not require high startup costs. One cannot own and maintain a slave for half the year. Perhaps, this reality reflected the high turnover of slave owners in Currituck County. Given this economic context, how did slavery shape the Currituck community context?

Currituck Community Context

In the 1850 and 1860 censuses, interviewers went door-to-door and assigned dwelling and household numbers according to the order of interview. They did so even when there was a distance between households. As a result, their enumerations were a rough approximation of next-door neighbors and community—people who might have known and interacted with one another. In Currituck County, it was common for free African Americans to live two or three dwellings if not next door to slave overseers, slaveholders, and their slaves. Also, in the census, some slaveholders, who employed free African Americans, listed them as part of their household. Free African Americans in White households might have been tenants living in separate quarters. If free Blacks were enumerated separately, the landowners would have had to pay a tax for having free Blacks living independently as tenants on their property. It was in owners' interest to make it seem that free African Americans living on their land were part of their household. Clearly, on the majority of the county's small farms, masters, slaves, and free Blacks worked side-by-side, lived on the same land, and had close relationships with one another (Franklin 1971, 196).

The County Court records and Deed books reveal other qualities about the economy and community in Currituck County. It showed a class of slave owners that escaped prior attention. These residents owned one to three slaves and had no apparent land or valuable property. Based on the age of household members, these were older residents whose slaves took care of them, did their housework, and enabled them to live well and independently. For these slave owners, slavery was about comfort, not profits. Much of the business of the court was settling the estates of these residents once deceased. The distribution of household property among heirs was remarkably thorough and meticulous. Relatives and others named in wills received the deceased property—i.e., two mirrors, three chairs, a cow, dresser, land, a mare, "two negroes named Sally and Tom," a sewing machine, and two horses. Slaves were mentioned casually as just another possession. Also, slaves were sold in whole, halves, or in quarters to settle debts.

Adult children in the court records and the deceased in their wills spoke affectionately about "the negroes" they sold, and of the years that these slaves gave of faithful service. The slaves sold had spent their lives caring for their masters, making them comfortable and often were themselves of advanced age. Other owners, who got into debt, paid it off by selling a Negro or two at public auctions, while Whites bought Negroes as investments for later sales to pay future debts. Still others hired out their slaves on contracts to do specific work. This was the routine business of the court in session after session, year after year.

Crime and Police

Slaves who violated the law or were found publically and repeatedly disruptive were ordered sold out of County (Currituck County June 1808). It did not matter whether their owner agreed to the sale or not. To commit a crime more severe than public disruption was to meet a more cruel fate. September 7, 1810, Negro Abraham was found guilty of felony and burglary and was hung the same day without the benefit of clergy until he was, in the words of the court, "dead, dead, dead." Furthermore, every district had night patrols appointed annually by the court. They searched for runaway slaves or slaves off the plantation or farm without permission. They made no distinction between slave and free. The court had to make rules for patrol conduct; the following are quotes of selective rules patrols had to follow that affected free African Americans (Currituck County August 1822):

- They should go through their district once in every fortnight as secret as possible to apprehend things.
- They are not to trouble no negro at preaching or prayer meeting . . . except if given the order to do so or they catch them on some misdemeanor.
- They are to give no negro more than 15 lashes with his shirt on that they catch them without a pass.
- They are to carry all the negroes they catch stealing or with stolen goods before the Justice of the Peace for judgment (they were not to hang negroes on their own).

Free African Americans were just as likely to be stopped by the patrols as slaves. By attending prayer services, Free African Americans could be accused of misdemeanors, just like slaves. Moreover, the patrols had no way to determine that a free African American without a pass was not a slave and should not be subject to 15 lashes, administered on the spot. Any African American, free or slave, could be accused of stealing and brought before the Justice of the Peace. Since free African Americans were no one's property, there would be fewer consequences if they were hung mistakenly or otherwise.

Currituck Racial Legal Context

What further reinforced free African Americans' invisibility was the North Carolina legislature's 21 laws passed specifically against free African Americans between 1790 and 1861. Provocations by free African Americans were not why these laws were passed. The response was laws passed due to White shock over David Walker's 1829 "Appeal in Four Articles" attacking slavery, and to the 1831 Slave Rebellion in nearby Southampton County, Virginia (Bogger 1997, 32, 68). The number of laws passed and their topics were a measure of the extent of White fear and insecurity over slavery and what they perceived as the increasing free African American menace in their midst. In a 13 year period alone, laws were passed to allow slaves to testify against free African Americans (1821), to bound-out "free negro" children (1827), against vagrancy by free African Americans (1827), against seditious (anti-slavery) publications (1829), against free African Americans marrying slaves (1830), against teaching negroes to read and write (1831), against "free negroes hawking and peddling goods" (1831), against free African Americans preaching in the presence of slaves (1831), "against negroes voting" (1835), against "teaching free negro apprentices to read or write" (1838), and against "negroes possessing and using all firearms" (1840).

Free African Americans in Currituck County

By 1850, life in Currituck County, like the three Virginia counties in the prior century, had become increasingly difficult. One indication is that four free African Americans for the first time were declared tax insolvents—William Hunt, Ivy Case, Henry Gregory, and Lemuel Gordon (Court Record, August 1857). All four were also originally from Virginia. Another indication of hard times was the number of free African American children and young adults who were bound out into White households by the 1850 census. If the poverty of free African Americans had not been broken by the Civil War and had continued, more free African American households would have had to flee elsewhere or faced economic and social collapse.

Invisibility: What is striking about the Currituck County Court, Deeds, and Census records is the extent that Bowsers and other free African Americans were rendered entirely invisible. None had court recorded wills, deeds, and contracts with others. They lived somewhere in each district; there were only four records in sixty years of free African

Americans buying or renting property. Undoubtedly, they paid taxes, but there are no records of their payments. The same invisibility from all written records was noted for Free African Americans in the South Carolina Piedmont (Megginson 2006, 59). Bounding out of free African American children as young as 18 months was the only area where they were not visible in court records. The court diligently reported the removal of these children from their families—especially Bowser and Hunt children. Furthermore, the parents' named in court records never appeared in the Census.

Virtually, all the Bowsers that appeared in the 1850 and 1860 Census were of children and young adults living in White households. Again, the names of the children in these White households did not match the names of children bound out earlier. There was official bounding out, but then there was as well an unregulated placement of free African American children and young adults in White households. Who and where were the unofficially bound-out children's parents; how did the children get into these White households? A partial answer to these questions came in the 1870 Census. African Americans who lived in the County for decades appeared in the census for the first time. Some had been slaves, but others were Free African Americans not counted in earlier censuses. While censuses are never 100 percent accurate, the extent to which free African Americans were missed between 1790 and 1860 suggests that they were left out intentionally. During slavery, it was just not necessary to count them.

Conclusion

Circumstances of African Americans freed in Virginia during the 1600s, such as the Bowsers, Cases, Hiters, and Thomas did not improve with the political changes after the American Revolutionary War and the transition of the British Colonies to the United States of America. Circumstances did not improve economically with the collapse of the tobacco economy by the 1790s. Free American Americans went from the promise of citizenship and the opportunity to prosper in Anthony Bowser's generation to the invisibility and the poverty of the female-headed households of Sarah and Mary Bowser in Currituck Country by 1800. From the Virginia colonial records, there appears to have been only four Bowser families during the 1700s able to rent sufficient land to earn enough money to purchase enslaved relatives, but they were the exceptions. Virginia became increasingly dependent on slavery and the repression of free African Americans and slaves alike.

Bowsers and other free African Americans who fled Virginia to Currituck County after 1790 were looking for some measure of relief from Virginia. What they found in North Carolina was the same. The restrictions they fled from in Virginia followed them. The fact that small farmers rather than large plantation owners dominated Currituck County may have brought some relief. Free Blacks found some work as farm-workers, house servants, and even work alongside slaves. Undoubtedly, free African Americans arrived at informal understandings with their White neighbors; they would be ignored as long as they remained invisible. An outcome is that their poverty and oppression continued into the 1800s in Currituck County.

Free African Americans farmers and workers had to be aware of every law passed against them, every act of abuse and discrimination, and every pitfall that awaited them. Indeed, they were acquainted with one another, socialized, exchanged news and rumors, devised strategies, and knew which Whites to do business with and whom to avoid. They visited each other, went to church together and frequented congregated in whatever roadhouses they were allowed to frequent. Having a racial identity and status in common did not mean that they were alike nor necessarily liked one another, but it did mean that their survival was dependent upon having at least a loose-knit community and keeping each other informed.

Psychological Burdens

The oppressive economic, community and legal contexts of eighteenth-century Virginia and Antebellum

North Carolina carried a psychological burden and called for resilience. After all, free African Americans lived in a fishbowl surrounded by Whites where one misstep at any time in eight generations could return them to slavery as well as cost their livelihood and their lives. Theirs was not an immigrant experience. They were part of the English-American culture from the beginning in Jamestown and knew it well—as outsiders. They were also part of an extended network of other free African Americans. How does one live in a pressure cooker for eight generations where the temperature and pressure build for two hundred years and then walk out alive? One can surmise. In their relationships with Whites, they had to be flexible in values, attitude, exercise tight control over emotions, and be very selective in body language as well as in how and what they said. They had to be very calculating and goal-oriented in their dealings with Whites and Blacks alike. Keeping some distance from others, even family, was better than familiarity. They depended as little as possible on others and were always vigilant for threats and dangers.

Such resilience over generations comes with a substantial cost. Chronic stress, elevated blood pressure, heart disease, strokes, alcoholism, and frequent colds and infections were likely outcomes—as was the case with slaves. However, there was also a social psychological cost evident in their relationships with other African Americans. Note that Free African Americans, like slaves, had difficulty getting along with one another. On Sundays and holidays to the dismay of observers, when slaves had "leisure" time together, there was a great deal of drinking, quarreling, fighting, cursing and swearing (Woods 1974, 272). There was a great deal of black-on-black violence, theft, and lack of regard and support for one another (Franklin 1971, 100). For example, a free African American, William Hamilton, was always pleasant with his White employer and strangers; he did not fight back even when White thugs accosted him. However, after taking refuge in a free African American woman's home, he went into a rage against her (Bogger 1997, 161).

By no means was he the only one to exhibit such behavior. In fact, in the Currituck County Court records, there was the spectacle of one free African American man suing another. Sidney Hunt and Jacob Spellman were together drinking, had a fight, and destroyed a great deal of furniture. The suit was for compensation. The plaintive won (Currituck County June 1802).

Much in Common

Recent literature on Free African Americans is about the triumph of individual family members who succeed against all the odds (Wolf 2012; Maris-Wolf 2015). These extraordinary people brought land, freed wives and children from slavery, started successful businesses, acquired educations, and earned the begrudging respect of Whites for their exceptional achievement. Such celebrations are needed. The same could be done for Bowsers by focusing solely on Anthony Bowser's early emancipation, and James Bowser, father and son's participation in the Revolutionary War. Then, there were the 34 Bowsers who fought in the Civil War and Benjamin Bowser's leadership at the Pea Island Rescue Station that was at the foundation of the US Coast Guard. Instead, the focus here has been on the essential questions about how they survived and persisted for eight generations during slavery.

Finally, the experiences of African Americans as slaves and as free people have so much in common that they are virtually indistinguishable in their outcomes in resilience and damage. The claim that one's people were "free" did not mean free African Americans did not experience the same conditions that oppressed slaves with the same outcomes. Perhaps, it is understandable why and how my father, raised in the early 1900s, would be ambivalent about his "free" past, about his family and Currituck County, much like a victim of trauma. He did not speak of the County or return until late in life, but, ultimately, was buried there.

BIBLIOGRAPHY

Ancestry.com. 2010. "Virginia, 1666 p. 50; U.S. and Canada, Passenger and Immigration Lists Index, 1500s–1900s." Ancestry.com.

Arnold, James N. 1884. "List of the names of the inhabitants of Barbados in the year 1638, who then possessed more than ten acres of land." *The Narragansett Historical Register.*

Atkins, Jonathan. 1988. *Census of the Island of Barbados, made in the year A.D. 1679.* Salt Lake City, Utah: Genealogical Society of Utah.

Bogger, Tommy L. 1997. *Free Blacks in Norfolk Virginia, 1790–1860.* Charlottesville: University Press of Viriginia.

Bowser, Addison Bartholomew. 1922. *The Bowser Family History.* Chicago: Excelior Printing Company.

Carbone, John S. 2001. *The Civil War in Coastal North Carolina.* Raleigh: The North Carolina Division of Archives and History.

Cecelski, David S. 2001. *The Waterman's Song: Slavery and Freedom in Maritime North Carolina.* Chapel Hill: University of North Carolina Press.

County, Currituck. 1790. *Deed Book No. 6, January 9.*

—. 1796. *Deed Book No. 8 December 6.*

Crow, Jeffrey J. 1977. *The Black Experience in Revolutionary North Carolina.* Raleigh: North Carolina Department of Cultural Resources.

Currituck County. August 1822. Minutes of the Court of Pleas and Quarter Sessions.

—. June 1802. Minutes of the Court of Pleas and Quarter Sessions.

—. June 1808. Minutes of the Court of Pleas and Quarter Sessions.

Earle, Carville. 1975. *The Evolution of a Tidewater Settlement System: All Hallow's Parish, Maryland, 1650–1783.* Vol. Research Paper 170. Chicago: The University of Chicago Department of Geography.

—. 1978. "A Staple Interpretation of Slavery and Free Labor." *Geographical Review* 68 (1): 51–65.

Fausz, J. Frederick. 2015. "Richard Bennett (bap. 1609–ca. 1675)." In *Dictionary of Virginia Biography,* edited by John G. Deal and Marianne E. Julienne. Richmond: Library of Virginia.

Franklin, John Hope. 1971. *The Free Negro in North Carolina, 1790–1860.* New York: W.W. Norton and Company.

Governor of Barbados. 1979. *The dispatches of govenor, Sir Jonathan Atkins, relating to the population of the island of Barbados, A.D. 1679–1680: comprising the names of the landowners, with the number of acres, of white sevants, and of negroes belonging to them, as well as other matter, including the nominal rolls of the regiments of the horse and foot soldiers belonging to the island.* Salt Lake City, Utah: Genealogical Societ of Utah.

Green, T.H., and Stephen Innes. 2005. *"Myne Owne Ground": Race and Freedom on Virginia's Eastern Shore, 1640–1676.* New York: Oxford University Press.

Heinegg, Paul. 2005. "Free African Americans of North Carolina, Virginia, and South Carolina from the Colonial Period to about 1820." Clearfield. http://www.freeafricanamericans.com/Beverly_Brogdom.htm.

—. 2009. *Free African Americans of North Carolina, Virginia, and South Carolina from the Colonial Period to About 1820.* 2 vols. Baltimore: Genealogical.com.

Herndon, Ruth Wallis, and John E. Murray. 2009. *Children Bound to Labor: The Pauper Apprentice System in Early America.* Ithaca: Cornell University Press.

Jackson, Luther Porter. 1971. *Free Negro Labor and Property Holding in Virginia, 1830–1860.* New York: Russell and Russell.

Kolchin, Peter. 1993. *American Slavery, 1619–1877.* New York: Hill and Wang.

Kulikoff, Allan. 1986. *Tobacco and Slaves: The Development of Southern Cultures in the Chesapeake, 1680–1800.* Chapel Hill: University of North Carolina Press.

Maris-Wolf, Ted. 2015. *Family Bonds: Free Blacks and Re-enslavement Law in Antebellum Virginia.* Chapel Hill: The University of North Carolina Press.

Megginson, W.J. 2006. *African American Life in South Carolina's Upper Piedmont, 1780–1900.* Columbia: University of South Carolina Press.

Morgan, Edmund S. 1975. *American Slavery, American Freedon: The Ordeal of Colonial Virginia.* New York: W.W. Norton and Company.

Principle Probate Registry. 1960. "Will of Richard Rennett." *Index of Wills P.C.C. 1676–1685* 10: 29.

Stuart, Andrea. 2013. *Sugar in the Blood: A Family Story of Slavery and Empire.* New York: Alfred A. Knopf.

Wagner, Anthony. 1966. *The Family of Bowser: Genealogical Researches with Particular Reference to Bowser of Yorkshire from Mediaeval Times.* London: MacLehose.

Wolf, Eva Sheppard. 2012. *Almost Free: A Story about Family and Race in Antebellum Virginia.* Athen: University of Georgia Press.

Woods, Peter H. 1974. *Black Majority: Negroes in Colonial South Carolina: From 1670 through the Stono Rebellion.* New York: Alfred A. Knopf.

Wright, Gavin. 1978. *The Political Economy of the Cotton South: Households, Markets, and Wealth in the Nineteenth Century.* New York: W.W. Norton.

Bowser Appendix

Free African Americans in Independent Households, Currituck County, N.C. 1790 to 1860 Censuses

1790	1800	1830	1850	1860
Charles Hunt	*Jonathan Case*	*Clark Gorden*	Isaac Wilson	George Baxter
James Boswell	Joseph Case	*Isam Hiter*	Clarky Garrett	Darcus Paterson
Sarah Bryan	*Sarah Smith*	*Joseph Gorden*	Tabitha Archy	Aldustus Archer
Price Dring	*Saml. Robins*	*Jacob Paterson*	Harvey Sawyer	A.J. Mercer
Mary Basnett	*Nancy Gordon*	*William Thomas*	Jno. Wilson	J. L. M. Garret
James Thomas	*Rachel Bowser*	*Jasper Hunt*	Biah Wilson	Alice Archer
Jonathan Case	Rachel Bennitt	*Salley Gorden*	Mary Walker	*Abba Wilson*
Hyram Hunt	*Dempsey Hunt*	*Joseph Thomas*	Chester Barcow	Alec Mercer
Demsey Hunt	John Hammonds	Judeth Luts	Grandy Case	*Fanny Case*
William Vever	Minies Turner	Hanner Blanchord	William Hunt	Caroline Barco
Edom Fuller	Wm. Chandler	Hanner Spelman	William Hunt	Elizabeth Gordan
Elizabeth Hitom (Hiter)	*Charles Hunte*	Joseph Jarves	Susan Gordon	Lovey Spilman
Peter Gordan	*Jeams Thomas*	*Jeremiah Gorden*	Fanny Hunt	Carolina Thomas
Charles Duglas	Wm. Pugh	Dempsey Gregory	Allen Sandling	Joseph Thomas
Bellar Turner	Sally Splman	*Joseph Case*	Amy Hiter	Betsy Gregory
Samson Turner	Wm. Dolleson	Sidney Hunt	Patsy Gordon	Aaron Gregory
Abi Jones	Jacob Supler	Ana Hiter	Joseph Thomas	Edney Patterson
Margaret Mekins	Thos. Spelman	Peter Gorden	William Thomas	Polly Gordan
Richard Mekins	Dennis Caps Sr.	John Cypress	Lidia Thomas	Dempsy Thomas
Mary Bathouse	Wm. Rogers	Caleb Wilson	Aron Thomas	Mary Sanderlin
Samuel Burnham	*Peggy Archer*	Daniel Wilson (4)	Henry Gregory	Alabama Sanderson
	Dolley Mydett	Byer Affrica	Pepperson Case	Ivy Case
N =21	Wm. Dollison(?)	David Crun	Dempsey Gregory	Betsy Marten
		Salley Bowser	James Thomas	James Bowser
	N = 23		William Paterson	Betsy Bowser
		N = 25	Nancy Paterson	Lydia Hunt
			Benjamin Bowser	Emily Hunt
				Amy Heighter
			N =27	Britany Thomas
				Asia Capps
				Benj. Bowser
				Catherine Bowser
				Daffany Bowser
				John P. Bowser
				N =34

1) 1800 and 1830 Free Others named in common with Whites deleted.
2) Names in *italic* are in Peter Heinegg's work for Virginia.

The Cumbo Family

TRACING ONE OF THE FIRST AFRICAN DESCENDED FAMILIES IN AMERICA

Luke Alexander and Andre Kearns

About the Cumbo Family

The Cumbo Family is one of the earliest documented families in America. Cumbo ancestors were among the first Africans arriving in Virginia prior to 1630. Over successive generations, many Cumbo family branches either maintained Black or mixed-race (mulatto) identities, passed into white communities (Melungeon, Portuguese or Irish) or fully embraced Native American (Lumbee, Tuscarora, Saponi or Meherrin) identities. Cumbo descendants today self-identify across all of these racial groups. Additionally, as the Cumbo family grew, so did variations of the name, which expanded to Cumba, Cumbee, Cumby, Cumbia, Combo, Cumber, McCumbee, and others.

On 18 April 1667, a Virginia land patent grants Emanuel Cumbo, "Negro," 50 acres in James City County. He obtains land formerly granted to William Davis.[1] This remarkable document makes Emanuel one of the few African-descended landowners in seventeenth-century Virginia.[2] It also raises important questions. How did he end up with his land? Where was he born? Who were his parents? Answering these questions reveals an inspiring story of an African man and woman's resilience and agency over bondage to create a free life for their Virginia-born son Emanuel Cumbo and future generations. To answer these questions, first we created the "Cumbo US South Y-DNA Project"[3] to trace our Cumbo family origins. Project results to date provide important clues to our Cumbo origins. We extensively researched early Virginia records, particularly land and patent records from 1619 to 1667.[4] Finally, we used a Virginia map from 1652[5] to identify the locations cited in the patents. These sources surfaced dots we connected to reveal our Cumbo family origin story.

Tracing African Origins

The first Africans in Virginia arrived from the Kingdom of Ndongo on the ships the *White Lion* and *Treasurer* (1619) and the *Fortune* (1628)[6] after being pirated from Portuguese slave ships. The Portuguese presence in Ndongo dates back to 1484.[7] The Portuguese attacked this kingdom in 1618 on a hunt to capture Africans to fuel the growing Portuguese slave trade.[8] "Cumbo US South Y-DNA Surname Project" participants mostly have African Haplogroups B and E, consistent with a family origin in Angola. A Y-DNA haplogroup is a genetic population group of people who share a common ancestor on their direct paternal line.

Table 1 Cumbo US South Y-DNA Participant Summary

Haplogroup	Participant Count	Surnames
B-M181	8	Cumbee, Cumbaa, Cumbea, Cumbie
E-M2	4	Cumbo, Cumber
R-M269	3	Cumbo, Combo

Note: As the Cumbo family grew in America, so did variation of the name which is represented in surnames participating in the project.

What's In a Name?

Emanuel Cumbo's parents were Emanuel and Joan from Ndongo. Their first names tie them to Portuguese-influenced Ndongo. Cumbo is a unique sounding name with origins in Africa. It is possibly derived from Kambol, the royal name of Ndongo.[9] Go to Google maps and you will locate a village in the north of Angola named Cumbo.[10] Search slave-trade records and you find hundreds of Cumbos, Combos, Kumbos, and Cumbahs from Angola, Cameroon, and Congo.[11]

Table 2   Representative Sample of Results from the African Origins Database Searching the Surname Cumbo

Name	Age	Gender	Ship Name
Cumbo	20	Male	San Antonia Milagroso
Combo	22	Female	Ucas
Combo	13	Male	Graca
Combo	24	Male	Faceirnha
Combo	13	Male	Maria
Combo	21	Male	Malaga of Belouru
Combo	8	Female	Si
Kumbo	7	Male	Laure
Cambo	8	Male	HCMS Princess Charlotte
Coombo	28	Female	Juan

Source: https://legacy.african-origins.org

The Cumbos in Virginia

Emanuel (father) and Joan were born around 1600 and 1610 in Ndongo.[12] They arrived in Point Comfort, Virginia sometime from 1619[13] and 1628.[14] From Point Comfort, they were bound to landowners at Archers Hope Creek in James City County, Virginia. In 1638, Richard Kemp lists "Emanuel, Negro" among numerous headrights[15] to secure 840 acres of land on Archers Hope Creek in James City County.[16] The next year, "Joan, a Negro" is listed among headrights for 1,200 acres to William Davis, Kemp's neighbor at Archers Hope Creek.[17]

Since Emanuel (father) and Joan arrived with no fixed-term indentured service contracts, they labored as bonded servants, enslaved in practice.[18] As they labored, slavery was rapidly forming in Virginia through custom, court rulings, and laws.[19] White landowners misused the headright system which was established in Virginia in 1618 to recruit labor for the colonies. Landowners exploited Africans like Emanuel and Joan as headrights by using them to secure new land holdings over and over without ever having to transfer land patents to them.

Emanuel (father) tried to escape his bondage for freedom. In 1640, he was serving William Pierce in York County which adjoins James City County. He hatched a plan to escape under the cover of night with six white servants. They all were caught sailing down the Elizabeth River to Norfolk. Emanuel was whipped, branded, and returned to bondage.[20] His dreams of freedom would have to be realized through his son.

The Life of Emanuel Cumbo (Son)

Emanuel Cumbo was born around 1634 to Emanuel (father) and Joan in James City County. His parents wanted him to have the freedom they were denied. They leveraged relationships with those for whom they labored over many years to petition the Virginia legislature for their son's freedom. They succeeded. In September 1644, the Virginia House of Burgess ruled the said servant "a Mulata named Manuel" was by the assembly adjudged no slave but to serve as other Christian servants [indentured servants] do and ordered to serve 21 years.[21]

Why might have Emanuel (son) been described as a mulatto in 1644? Note that this descriptor is an outlier relative to other descriptions of him and his parents. Africans represent a broad spectrum of complexions. Emanuel and/or Joan could have also been of mixed Portuguese ancestry.

On 18 April 1667, two years after Emanuel Cumbo (son) was freed from his twenty-one-year bondage, he took ownership of fifty acres of land in Archers Hope Creek where his mother and father labored. Cumbo obtained his property from land formerly deeded to William Davis, who had listed Emanuel's mother, Joan, among the headrights required to claim it in 1639, and adjoining land owned by Richard Kemp, who listed his father, Emanuel, as a headright in 1638.

By September 1667, the Virginia Assembly declared baptism does not free enslaved people.[22] Had Emanuel Cumbo's timeline shifted a few years, perhaps he would not have achieved freedom. But he did, making him and his descendants free people in America from that point forward.

Cumbo Family Timeline and Locations

The letters [A–D] connect events to locations on the map of Virginia, found below the timeline.

1619/1628: Africans Emanuel and Joan arrive from Ndongo on the *White Lion*, *Treasurer*, or *Fortune* to Point Comfort, VA. [A]

1638: Patent places Emanuel at Archers Hope Creek in James City, VA [B]

> RICHARD KEMP, Esqr., 840 acs., called the meadowes neare unto the Rich Neck upon Archers hope Cr. purchased by sd. Kemp of Georg Minifye, Merchant; 4 Mar. 1638, p. 627. Beg. at the horse path over against part of the sd. Rich Neck, N. N. W. downe the side of the meadowes to a br. of Powhetan Sw. &c. 50 acs. due for his own per. adv. & 800 acs. for trans, of 16 pers: Henry Fenton, Thomas Cooke, Robert Sumers, John How, Georg Harrison, Francisco, Mingo, Maria, Mathew, Peter, Cosse, old Gereene, Bass, young Peter, Paule, Emmanuell, Negroes.

1639: Patent places Joan at Archers Hope Creek in James City near Emanuel; ties her to William Davis. [B]

> WILLIAM DAVIS, 1,200 acs. James City Co., June 28, 1639, page 661. N. upon land of Lt. Richard Popely, S. upon Capt. Humphry Higginson, W. upon head of Archers Hope Cr. E. toward bryery Swamp. Due for trans, of 24 pers: Sarah Browne, Isaac, Andrew Howell, Ann Keeding, Nicho. Goldsmith, Wm. Burfur, Thomas Thorrogood, John Barker, Morgan Williams, Wm. Davis, Richard Shaw, John Badden, Abigail Drewry, Richard Vardall, Mathew Burrow, Tho. Floyd, John Peirce, Richard Prichard, Joan, a Negro.

1640: Court records place Emanuel in York near James City attempting to escape bondage. [C]

> "They set off on a 'Saturday night,' and by the time they were apprehended they had sailed a considerable distance down the Elizabeth River … Emanuel the Negro; was given thirty stripes, a letter 'R' burnt into his cheek, and shackling for at least a year."

1642: Patent places Emanuel in bondage in York. [C]

> WILLIAM IRELAND and ROBERT WALLIS, 700 acs. Yorke Co., July 13, 1642, Page 812. At the head of St. Andrews Creek, N. E. upon Joseph Croshaw & Richard Maior. Trans, of 14 pers.: Rebecca, wife of Robert Wallis, Emanuella a Negroe, … [23]

1651: Patent ties Joan and Emanuel (son) together in Northumberland County adjacent to Richard Bushrod and William Smith properties. [D]

> RICHARD TURNEY, 2,109 acs. Northumberland Co., 8 July 1651, p. 333. Abutting Sly. upon Potomeck Riv., Ely. upon a great marsh, Wly. upon a bay, & Nly. upon a creek issueing out of sd. bay. … Trans, of 42 pers: … Syon the Turke, Manuell the Negro, Joane the Negro. … [24]

1665: Virginia House of Burgess record states that Emanuel Cumbo (son), formerly owned by Thomas Bushrod [Richard's brother] and William Smith, is freed from bondage.

> To the Honourable Sr Wm. Berkley Knight Governor &c. And the Honourable Council of Virginia. he humble petition of Wm. Whittacre Sheweth. That he formerly bought of Mr. Thomas Bushrod a Mulata named Manuel who bought him of Colo. Wm. Smith's Assignee as a Slave for Ever but in September 1644 the said Servant was by the Assembly adjudged no Slave and but to serve as other Christian servants do and was freed in September 1665. Your petitioner most humbly

prays he may have satisfaction from the Levy being freed by the Country and bought by your Petitioner at 25 Sterling.[25]

1667: Patent grants Emanuel Cumbo (son) fifty acres at Archers Hope Creek, secured by William Davis for Joan's headright. [B]

To all who read now known great hand of Will Berkeley Knight Good Governor Grants Emanuell Cumbo Negro fifty acres of land according to his ancient landfall Bounties claimed On lands in James City VA Colony said bounty lands being part of a greater record it has formerly granted unto Will Davis lately found to escheat to his majesty's crown in Virginia whom found at Will of your jury Has ordered wherein attest faith of Col. Myles Cary Esq General Minister Escheat Grant fault a County and the Jury sworn afore affirm
Found and appeared here this 18th Day of April 1667 may approve deed is now
Granted unto the said Emanuell who has made his composition so has paid awarding
Found so judge and assign his so to lands ordering and filing
Deed this 18th day of April 1667.

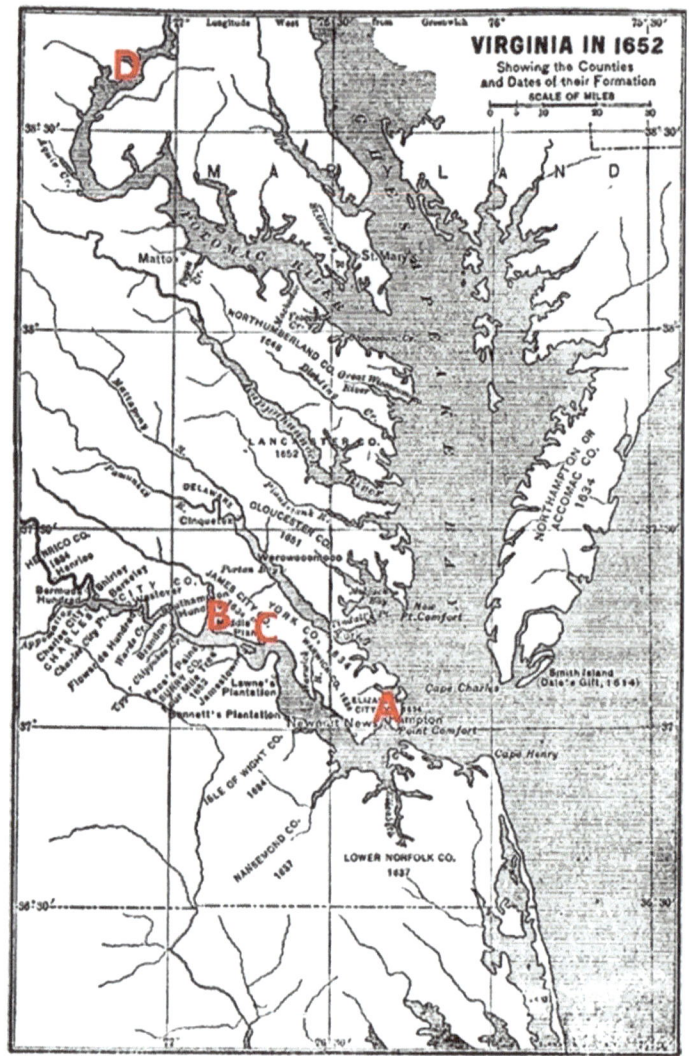

Table 3 African Population in Early Virginia[26]

Year	African Population
1619	32
1624	22
1640	150
1649	300
1671	2,000

Note: The African population in early Virginia was very small, so references to the same names found in early patent records for similar locations likely reference the same people.

Addressing Alternative Theories

Now that we have presented our Cumbo family origin story, we would like to address three alternative theories of Cumbo origin that are in the public domain.

Theory #1. Could Emanuel Cumbo be the son of European Hugh Davis and an African woman? This theory is based on a 1630 resolution sentencing Hugh Davis to be publicly whipped for "lying with a negro."[27] It assumes a connection between Hugh Davis and William Davis based on a shared surname to explain why Emanuel ended up with the land formerly owned by William Davis. Here is our counter: Our Cumbo Y-DNA project points to paternal origins in Africa and not Europe. Also note none of our participants generate Davis matches. Additionally, we have established the connection between Emanuel Cumbo and William Davis through patent records.

Theory #2. Could Emanuel Cumbo (father) be one of the 1619 "twenty and odd" who were bound to Abraham Piersey?[28] Here is our counter: The

African Emanuel could have absolutely been one of the twenty and odd, but he was not bound to Piersey. We know this because the African men listed on Piersey's plantation were named and Emanuel was not one of them.[29] He could have been one of the nine unnamed Africans in the 1623 Virginia census, but at this point we do not know for sure. So all we can really say with certainty is that he is one of the first Africans.

Theory #3. Is it possible that references to Emanuel (father) prior to 1667 are of Emanuel Driggers? The African Emmanuel Driggers was born around 1620 and bound to Francis Pott on his plantation in Magotha Bay, Northampton County, Virginia.[30] We counter that they were two different people and use geography to support this theory. Emanuel Cumbo (father) and Emanuel Driggers both disembarked at Point Comfort, Virginia. From there Emanuel Driggers went to Northampton County, Virginia, on the eastern shore, where he lived his life; Emanuel (father) lived their lives west of the Chesapeake in James City and York County Virginia.

Call to Action

This is a family story of African strength, resilience, and agency over bondage uncovered through Y-DNA test results, early Virginia records, and places. Our Cumbo family research continues through the "Cumbo US South Y-DNA Project." If you are a male Cumbo, Combo, Cumbee, Cumby, Cumbea, Cumber, or any other surname derivative, please consider joining our "Cumbo US South Y-DNA Project." Note that African-descended Cumbos identify across all racial designations.

Learn more about our project here: https://www.familytreedna.com/groups/cumbo-us-south/about.

About the Authors

Luke Alexander and Andre Kearns are Cumbo descendants who have researched their family roots extensively. A DNA connection brought them and their Cumbo branches together.

Table 4 Cumbo Pedigree for Luke Alexander and Andre Kearns

Emanuel (B. abt. 1600) & Joan (B. abt. 1610)
Ndongo

Emanuel Cumbo
B. abt. 1634
James City County, VA

Richard Cumbo
B. abt. 1667
Charles City, VA

Gideon Cumbo
B. abt. 1702
New Kent, VA

Cannon Cumbo B. abt 1730/5 North Carolina	Elizabeth Cumbo B. abt. 1728 Virginia
Stephen Cumbo B. abt. 1755 North Carolina	Cannon Cumbo B. abt. 1758 Brunswick, VA
Mary Polly Cumbo B. 1802 Robeson County, NC	Britton Cumbo Sr. B. 1776/96 Northampton County, NC
Calvin Lowery B. 15 Jan 1835 Robeson County, NC	Britton Cumbo Jr. B. 1825 Northampton County, NC
Annie Bell Lowery B. 3 Dec 1864 Robeson County, NC	Matthias Cumbo B. 1845 Northampton County, NC
Cecil Bell Spaulding B. 1 Jun 1909 Columbus County, NC	Elizabeth Florence Cumbo B. 1866 Northampton County, NC
Mother of Luke Alexander	Sarah Ann Biggs B. 15 Aug 1902 Suffolk, VA
Luke Alexander	James Edward Richards B. 30 Aug 1920 Suffolk VA

ENDNOTES

1. *Virginia's Land Patent Collection*, Patent book No. 6 1666–1679, p. 39.
2. Martha W. McCartney, *A Study of the Africans and African Americans on Jamestown Island and at Green Spring, 1619–1803*, p. 245.
3. https://www.familytreedna.com/groups/cumbo-us-south/about
4. Nell Marion Nugent, *Cavaliers and Pioneers: Abstracts of Virginia Land Patents and Grants*.
5. Albert Bushnell Hart, LL.D., *The American Nation* Vol. 4 (New York, NY: Harper and Brothers, 1906), p. 98.
6. K. I. Knight, *Unveiled: The Twenty & Odd, Documenting the First Africans in England's America 1619–1625*, pp. 107–111.
7. Chisholm, Hugh, ed. (191), Angola. *Encyclopædia Britannica*. 2 (11th ed.), Cambridge University Press. pp. 38–40.
8. Rein, Lisa (3 September 2006). "Mystery of Va.'s First Slaves Is Unlocked 400 Years Later," *Washington Post*.
9. Tim Hashaw, *The Birth of Black America: The First African Americans and the Pursuit of Freedom at Jamestown*.
10. maps.google.com
11. https://legacy.african-origins.org/
12. Emanuel and Joan's birth dates are estimates based on the dates of patent records that reference them and average life expectancy of people in the 1600s in Virginia.
13. Olivia Waxman, "The First Africans in Virginia Landed in 1619. It Was a Turning Point for Slavery in American History—But Not the Beginning" (Aug 20, 2019), *Time Magazine*.
14. "Virginia in 1628," *The Virginia Magazine of History and Biography*, 7 (1900), p. 265.
15. The headright system began in Jamestown in 1618. It was designed to solve labor shortages created by the growing tobacco economy. Headrights patented fifty acres to anyone who would pay for the transportation costs of a laborer. Sponsors could pay for the passage of a laborer. Travel debts were paid off through indentured servant contracts. Land patents were conveyed to laborers after their terms of indentured service were completed.
16. Nell Marion Nugent, *Cavaliers and Pioneers: Abstracts of Virginia Land Patents and Grants* (19434), Patent Book No. 1—Part II, p. 104.
17. Ibid., p. 112.
18. Robyn Sidersky, Gordon Rago and Saleen Martin, "Here's what historians have to say about Northam's 'indentured servants' Comment" (Feb. 11, 2019), *The Virginia Pilot*.
19. John Henderson Russell, *The Free Negro in Virginia, 1619–1865*, pp. 18–19.
20. Stephen Innes and T. H. Breen, *Myne Owne Ground*, p. 29.
21. *Journals of the House of Burgess for Virginia 1659/60–1663*, p. 34.
22. "An act declaring that baptisme of slaves doth not exempt them from bondage" (1667), www.encyclopediavirginia.org.
23. Nugent, *Cavaliers and Pioneers*, Patent Book No. 1—Part II, p. 133.
24. Ibid., Patent Book No. 2 p. 218.
25. *Journals of the House of Burgess for Virginia 1659/60–1663*, p. 34.
26. Anastasia Harman, Natalie D. Cottrill, Paul C. Reed, and Joseph Shumway, *Documenting President Barack Obama's Maternal AfricanAmerican Ancestry: Tracing His Mother's Bunch Ancestry to the First Slave in America*, p. 18.
27. Knight, *Unveiled: The Twenty & Odd*, p. 86.
28. Blog by Jim Farmer, "Pioneers Along the Southern Trails, Emanuel and Joan Cumbo of Colonial Virginia" (Feb 15, 2020).
29. Susan Myra Kingsbury, *Records: 1624–1625 Muster of Virginia*, Vol. 3.
30. Paul Heinegg, FreeAfricanAmericans.com, Driggers Family.

Andre Kearns is a genealogist, public speaker, commentator, and writer with deep roots in the American south and a passion for discovering new ancestors and learning their stories. As an African American, he knew he descended from enslaved persons and likely slave owners, which DNA analysis helped  confirm. Through his research, he also discovered ancestors who were free people of color long before the Civil War, Native Americans, and multiracial persons. Discovering this ancestry has unlocked previously unknown rich aspects of American history. Andre has been a genealogist for fifteen years. He holds an MBA from Harvard Business School and a BA from Morehouse College. He regularly shares his Cumbo family research findings at www.Cumbofamily.com. He also blogs on Race, Culture, History and Genealogy at www.medium.com under the name Andre Kearns.

Luke Alexander is a genealogist and community historian with a focus on African American and Indigenous heritage in the Carolinas. He serves as vice-president of the Benjamin & Edith Spaulding Descendants Foundation, Inc., and he is engaged in phil-  anthropic activities in his ancestral hometown of Farmers Union, North Carolina. Luke shares direct ancestry from several of the earliest recorded families of African origin in America, along with direct descent from the Lumbee, Waccamaw, and Cape Fear Native American nations. He is a founding administrator of the Carolinas FPOC DNA Project and Cumbo US South DNA Project hosted by FTDNA, as well as coordinator of the Lumbee Indians DNA Project and Cape Fear-Waccamaw Heritage Project hosted by GEDmatch.

2021 Family Salutes

Commemorate your family with a full-page ad in the 2021 *AAHGS Journal*

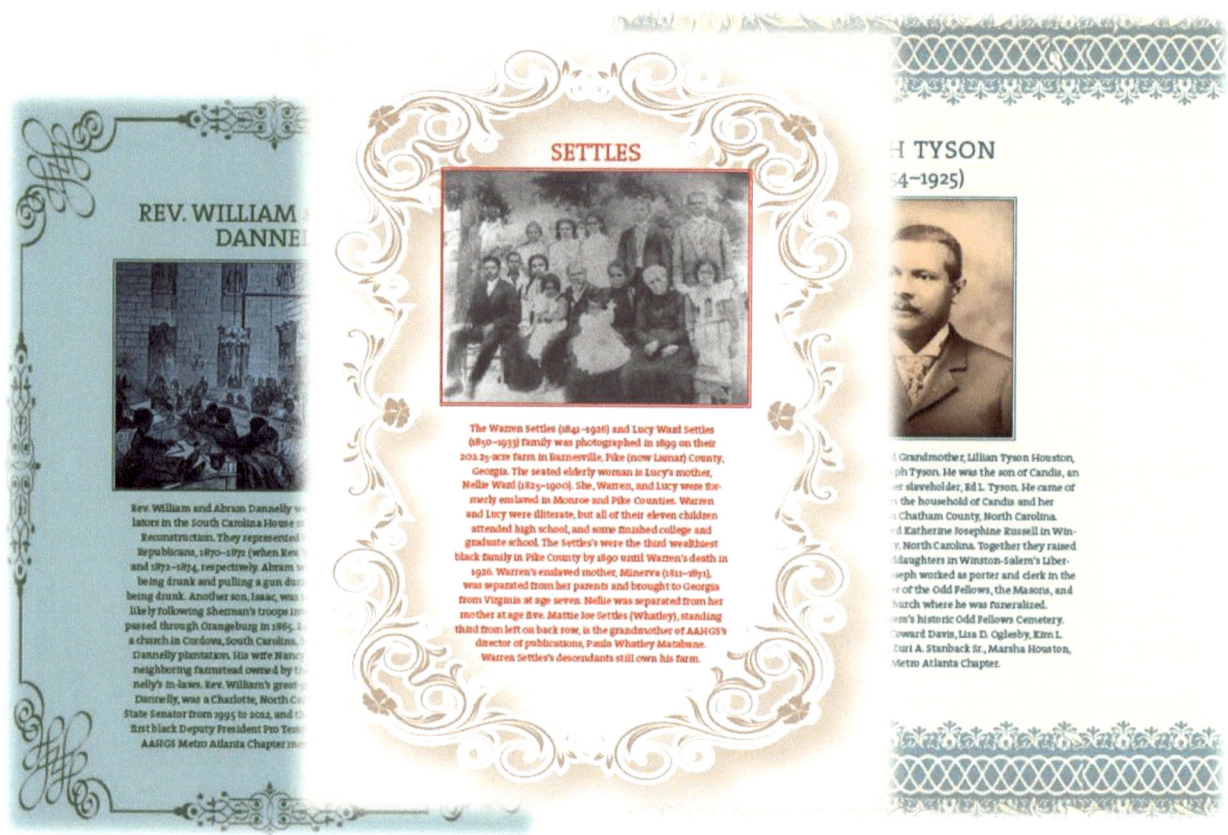

Email Journal@aahgs.org for more information

City of Renaissance: Frederick Douglass's Baltimore

Donna Tyler Hollie, PhD

In an 1846 letter to abolitionist William Lloyd Garrison, Frederick Douglass wrote:

> Though I am more closely connected and identified with one class of outraged, oppressed and enslaved people, I cannot allow myself to be insensible to the wrongs and sufferings of any part of the great family of man. I am not only an American slave, but a man, and as such, am bound to use my powers for the welfare of the whole humanbrotherhood.[1]

In *The North Star* of 28 July 1848, Douglass wrote:

> Standing as we do upon the watch-tower of human freedom, we cannot be deterred from an expression of our approbation of any movement, however humble, to improve and elevate the character and condition of any members of the human family.[2]

These are the words of a moral, honorable and humane man. Remarkably, these are the words of a man who, during his formative years, lived under an immoral, dishonorable and inhumane system—American slavery. In 1838, Frederick Douglass escaped from slavery. That he was also able to escape victimization by the system is extraordinary. How was he able to emerge from slavery with his spirit unscathed? What were the circumstances which shaped his ideology and impacted his ability to make contributions of lasting importance to the human family?

It was in March 1826 that a boy, approximately eight years old, then known as Frederick Augustus Washington Bailey, arrived in Baltimore. Sent by his owner to be a slave to Hugh Auld, he was to spend nine of his youthful years in Maryland's largest city. It was here that the life altering aspects of literacy became apparent to Douglass and where he learned how to read, write and do basic arithmetic. Baltimore was the site of his religious conversion and the place where he began to seriously question why some people were enslaved and others not. In Baltimore, he acquired a marketable skill, began to develop oratorical proficiency, formed productive friendships, met Anna Murray who would become his first wife and planned his escape from slavery.

As a child living on a plantation owned by of one of Maryland's wealthiest families, Douglass observed and was puzzled by the disparity in the circumstances of whites and Blacks. He believed instinctively that the inequality and cruelty of his environment were not the natural order and he determined that the dominance of one group by another was morally wrong.

The institution of slavery demanded submissiveness, a trait uncharacteristic of young Douglass. As an intelligent, inquisitive, assertive slave, Douglass would have had difficulty surviving plantation slavery.[3] Fortunately, he did not spend his formative years in the repressive environment of plantation slavery. It was the unique quality of his experiences in Baltimore which were of primary importance in the transformation of Frederick Bailey, slave, to Frederick Douglass, champion of the rights of the "whole human brotherhood." This paper examines Douglass's sojourn in Baltimore, emphasizing the Fells Point community and the influences of slaves and free Blacks on his evolution to freedman.

On the Lloyd plantation, Douglass was inadequately fed and clothed, emotionally and physically neglected, abused and subjected to ridicule and innuendo regarding his unidentified white father. In his autobiographical writings, he vividly describes several acts of exploitation and torture perpetrated by whites, the impact it had on the slaves who endured it and the fears he, a vulnerable child, experienced as a result. He presented a poignant account of his brief encounters with his mother, Harriet. Due to her residence on a distant plantation and her death at an early age, Douglass was unable to form emotional bonds with her.

The atmosphere in the Baltimore home of Hugh and Sophia Auld was vastly different and a radical improvement over that of Douglass's owner Aaron Anthony. For the first time in his life, he was physically well-cared for, receiving regular, sufficient and nourishing meals, adequate clothing and was provided with decent sleeping quarters. More importantly, Sophia Auld provided the nurturing that social scientists maintain is essential for the development of a positive self-image, confidence and emotional security necessary for success. The daughter of working class, devout Methodists who subscribed wholeheartedly to their denominational tenet that slavery was contrary to the will of God, Sophia had been employed as a weaver prior to her marriage and had never interacted with enslaved people. She related to Douglass not as a slave but as a motherless child. While Douglass never specifically stated that Sophia showed him love, he indicated that she treated him kindly, providing him with friendship, comfort, moral training and self-confidence. Additionally, Sophia discouraged the downcast countenance deliberately inculcated in enslaved people and admonished him frequently, "Don't be afraid."[4] It was from such treatment that Douglass became secure in his worth as a human being.

Sophia Auld provided Douglass with another gift which he would cherish and use for the remainder of his life. Having previously developed a fascination with the printed word, Douglass credits Sophia's melodious reading of the book of Job with intensifying his desire for literacy. At his request, she taught him the alphabet and to read and spell small words; unlike other slave holding states, this practice was not illegal in Maryland.[5] Typifying the reaction of a mother/teacher, Sophia proudly discussed Douglass's accomplishments with her husband. When Hugh Auld prohibited the lessons, fearing that Douglass would become discontent with his status as a slave, Douglass recognized literacy as a liberating mechanism and, with clever determination, devised various strategies for learning to read. He used bribery and clever ruses to induce his white playmates and co-workers on the docks to share their knowledge of reading.[6] He also scavenged for discarded printed materials which he hid and labored over in the privacy of his room. Much of what he found inflamed his interest in liberation. For the remainder of his life, he used the printed word not just for his own pleasure but also in his quest for equality and justice for all people.

Had he remained on the Lloyd plantation, Douglass would have been trained at an early age for the intense labor which was the lot of most male slaves. In Baltimore, his primary responsibility was to be a companion for two-year-old Tommy Auld, an association which resulted in an emotional bond between the two boys. Douglass was given other responsibilities commensurate with his age such as running errands and obtaining the family's daily supply of water from the town pump. This left time for playing in the streets of Fells Point with boys of his age group. Usually the only Black child in the group, Douglass experienced no disparate treatment and concluded that color prejudice was not an inherent human characteristic, but learned behavior. He realized that behavior which is learned can be unlearned, a belief that must have sustained him in his efforts to abolish slavery and promote the concept of equality for Blacks and women.

The first of three Fells Point residences Douglass shared with the Aulds was a two-story frame house on the corner of Aliceanna Street and Happy Alley, now Durham Street. Located near Baltimore's harbor, Fells Point was home to a thriving shipbuilding industry and was a busy international port. Hugh Auld, a carpenter, worked in the shipbuilding industry as did most of the men, Black, white, slave and free, in the neighborhood. Blacks dominated the caulking trade, considered semi-skilled work, because they were excluded from trades such as carpentry and sail making.[7] In the year following Douglass's arrival in Baltimore, 39 percent of Blacks were laborers employed as draymen, sawyers and porters. Free Blacks were frequently independent businessmen who worked as barbers, caterers and hack drivers. Black women were employed as laundresses, domestic servants in private homes and hotels and street vendors.[8] On the plantation Douglass observed that some white people, although idle, prospered as a result of the labor of others. In Fells Point, he saw few idle rich people; he saw instead people of various races, classes and genders supporting themselves by their own labor.

The community was ethnically and culturally diverse. The Auld's neighbors were of German, French, English, Scotch, Irish and African origins. Free Blacks were often clustered in the small alley streets where the houses were often no more than twelve feet wide, while the whites lived, with slaves, in larger homes on main thoroughfares. Some free Blacks, like the prosperous barber John Fernandis, were Brazilian immigrants.[9] People of Haitian descent, refugees from the 1793 revolution, were also residents. Sailors of various nationalities were visible in the neighborhood. From his observation of and interaction with this diverse population, a boy as astute as Douglass recognized that, in spite of physical and cultural differences, there were commonalities in the human experience.

Slavery in Baltimore differed from slavery on Maryland's Eastern Shore, site of Douglass's birth. Instances of inhumanity which Douglass witnessed in Fells Point were the exception rather than the rule. In an urban setting, negative behavior is more easily observed and more likely to draw public censure than in isolated, rural communities. In addition, Douglass heard Sophia Auld's frequently expressed disapproval of the cruelty of the slave trade, an opinion he would not likely have heard on the Lloyd plantation.

The religious and social climate of Fells Point fostered a more humane treatment of slaves. Baltimore was a center of religious opposition to slavery and home to active antislavery organizations.

The Methodist denomination, to which Sophia belonged and Douglass joined, had long been influential in the city. Lovely Lane Church, considered the mother church of American Methodism, was established in Fells Point in 1774. In 1780 and 1784, conferences were held at which prohibitions against slave ownership by church members were established. Methodist preachers "Black Harry" Hoosier and Richard Allen, the founder of the A.M.E. church, were prominent individuals who participated in these conferences.[10] While the prohibitions were not universally adopted or enforced and while Blacks were not afforded full equality within the church, the expectation of humane treatment was deeply ingrained in the church's ideology.

The nation's fourth antislavery society was founded in Baltimore in 1798. Included in its membership were the city's most prominent businessmen and civic leaders, with Methodists and Quakers in the majority. Free Blacks were active participants in the antislavery movement as well. Ministers such as Daniel Coker frequently expressed abolitionist sentiments from the pulpit. In 1830, Coker, Hezekiah Grice, a free Black butcher and William Watkins, a free Black teacher, formed the National Convention of the Free People of Color. The purpose of the group was to provide a forum for the discussion of issues important to the entire Black community and to present the community's concerns in a unified voice.

As a result of a dispute between Thomas Auld, who owned Douglass, and Hugh Auld, Douglass was sent to St. Michael's, Maryland in 1833. For a three-year period he once again experienced harsh and brutal slavery amid unsuccessful efforts to mold him into an acquiescence. Returning to Baltimore, he found many changes. There had been a rapid increase in the number of Irish immigrants and in the number of free Blacks migrating from rural areas. Many of the immigrants were uneducated and poor. The result was increased competition for unskilled, lower paying jobs and increased acts of discrimination and violence directed by the Irish toward Blacks. Douglass was the victim of a vicious physical assault by racist white co-workers. The fact that neither he nor Hugh Auld could seek redress from the law was another circumstance fueling his determination to be free.

Tommy Auld, perhaps having absorbed the racism prevalent in the neighborhood, no longer related to Douglass as an older, beloved brother. Douglass was no longer a little boy in need of nurturing and his relationship with Sophia became strained, much like the changes occurring between mothers and teenaged sons asserting their independence. Hugh Auld, who had never prospered economically, had failed at his attempt to establish a shipbuilding business and was drinking excessively. Resenting the financial expense of supporting a young man and recognizing Douglass's potential for generating income, Auld apprenticed Douglass to a caulker. Douglass became adept at his trade and was able to take advantage of a unique feature of Baltimore slavery, hiring out.

Baltimore's economy was not dependent on slavery. As the cost of living increased in Baltimore, ownership of slaves became economically impractical for many. Between 1810 and 1830, slave ownership began to decline; by 1850, only about 1 percent of the population owned slaves.[11] Many owners had inherited them from relatives in rural areas. Such slaves were liabilities as the cost of their upkeep was greater than the income generated. To compensate for financial losses, owners found employment for their slaves among non-slave holding people. Some affluent citizens, seeking enhanced status, hired slaves as domestics and carriage drivers. Many, like Douglass, worked at the docks. Hired slaves submitted a portion of their wages to the owners and were required to provide for their own food and shelter. The owner realized a profit while the advantage to the slave was a degree of autonomy unheard of in rural areas. For Douglass the experience of being hired led to his enjoying some of the privileges of freedom and enhanced his desire to be permanently free.

Douglass was responsible for finding work and negotiating for wages. He was able to earn as much as nine dollars weekly, could present the required six dollars to Hugh Auld and could apply the remaining three dollars to food, shelter, clothing, reading material and savings. In short, he lived as a free man. Additionally, his interaction with members of the free Black community escalated, serving to broaden his religious, educational and cultural horizon and re-enforcing his belief that his own freedom was attainable. Fear that their slaves would develop this optimistic attitude led many rural owners to prohibit interaction between slaves and free Blacks.

Six years before Douglass's initial arrival in Baltimore, there were 4,357 slaves and 10,326 free Blacks. Four years later, there were 4,120 slaves and 14,790 free Blacks.[12] Among the free Black population there were 1,488 slave owners in 1820, and 2,423 in 1830.[13] Often Black slave owners had purchased relatives in order to prevent whites from selling them away. Substantial in number, some of Baltimore's free Blacks were prosperous and many were proactive in improving the quality of life for the entire community. Unlike New Orleans which also had a substantial free Black population, Blacks in Baltimore were less socially stratified. Consequently, many slaves participated in and benefited from the educational, religious, and other uplift activities initiated by free Blacks. Douglass availed himself of these opportunities.

Education was paramount for this community and during Douglass's residence approximately fifteen schools were established and operated by Baltimore Blacks.[14] Although taxed, free Blacks were denied access to the public schools which opened in 1829.[15] Churches, of various denominations, took compensatory action. In 1809, Daniel Coker, the first bishop in the African Methodist Episcopal Church, taught at the African Academy on Sharp Street.[16] Established in 1802, the Academy was a religious and educational institution, a dual role replicated throughout the Black community. One hundred and fifty tuition paying students, some residents of Washington, D.C., were enrolled by 1820.[17] In 1815, the first free school in Baltimore opened at St. Patrick's Church, where classes were open to poor children of all races.[18] Within a year of offering lessons to the children of Bethel A.M.E. church, Pastor Daniel Payne, later to become an A.M.E. bishop, was operating a school in Fells Point with fifty students. Haitian women, founders of the Oblate Sisters of Providence, the world's first order of Black nuns, taught in Fells Point prior to 1828.

Secular community members operated schools also. In 1825, William Lively operated both day and night schools where he provided, for a fee, classical education. In his Sabbath School, he provided, at no charge, religious instruction. Like Lively, William Watkins offered musical instruction and classical courses at the Watkins Academy where his niece, poet/abolitionist Frances Ellen Watkins Harper taught. Also indicative of the community's support for education is the $3,500.00 bequest in the will of a free Black man, Nelson Wells, which was to be used to promote the intellectual improvement of Black children who could not afford tuition.[19]

Douglass attended classes at the Sabbath school at Dallas Street Methodist Church and also taught there. It is significant to note that while Hugh Auld verbally opposed Douglass's efforts to learn to read, he took no action to prohibit his attendance at school. This act of tolerance was at the mid-point of the attitudes of white Baltimoreans toward Black literacy. Other whites, such as Quaker merchant Elisha Tyson and Roman Catholic priest Father Joubert provided both financial and emotional support. Many Baltimore businessmen sought literate employees as the following advertisement indicates: "WANTED—A colored man, to act as Porter. None need apply unless they can read, write and understand figures."[20]

Douglass was associated with at least three Baltimore churches—Sharp Street Memorial United Methodist, Centennial-Caroline United Methodist and Bethel A.M.E.—all of which proudly claim him as a member.[21] These churches offered spiritual, educational and charitable services to Blacks, slave and free. In addition, they were culturally and politically active. As early as 1826, Sharp Street and Bethel were hosting public debates on the merits of colonization and the strategies of various abolitionists.[22] At Dallas Street, forerunner of Centennial-Caroline, Douglass heard his first lecture by an educated Black man, Dr. Lewis G. Wells. Following a sermon at Bethel by lay preacher Charles Johnson, Douglass was converted to Christianity. He shared with attorney/educator Richard T. Greener his pride in hearing intelligent Blacks speak at Sharp Street Church. All three congregations separated from white churches in protest of discriminatory practices such as relegating Blacks to balcony seating, serving communion only after whites were served and limiting Blacks' opportunities to rise to positions of authority.

Through his involvement in these churches, Douglass developed beneficial friendships. At Bethel he formed a relationship with Charles Lawson. A free Black employed as a drayman, "Uncle" Lawson was Douglass's spiritual mentor. With limited literacy Lawson depended on Douglass to read scriptures for him which he, Lawson, interpreted. Thus he helped enhance Douglass's literacy. In direct defiance of Hugh Auld's wishes, Douglass spent a great deal of time with Lawson, accompanying him to prayer meetings and to church services. There he was exposed to the effective oratorical styles of Black preachers such as Nathaniel Peck and Edward Waters. Peck, who advocated emigration to Guiana, would later join with other clergy to lead the fight for publicly funded schools for Black Baltimoreans.[23] Waters would become the third bishop in the A.M.E. church.[24]

The friendship between Douglass and John W. Locks began either at Bethel, where Locks was an active member, or at the docks where both were caulkers. Born free, Locks established a successful hack and funeral business and was a founder of the Chesapeake Marine Railway and Dry Dock Company, America's first Black owned shipyard. Locks was one of the first Blacks to serve on a federal jury and was a leader in the 1880 fight to secure employment of Black teachers in Black public schools. Newspaper accounts support John Locks' descendants' description of his close relationship with Douglass.[25]

At Dallas Street Methodist Church, Douglass became acquainted with Henry and Isaac Rolles. Isaac, a hack driver and reputedly an agent for the Underground Railroad, carried Douglass's baggage to the train station on the day he claimed his freedom[26]. Henry, five other young free Black men and Douglass formed the East Baltimore Mental Improvement Society, a debating club. Membership increased but Douglass remained the only slave. He frequently expressed in meetings, which were held in various homes in Fells Point, his desire for freedom and his intent to rise to a position of authority and power, specifically that he would become a United States senator.[27] In addition to sharpening his intellectual and oratorical skills, the club provided several other benefits for Douglass. Here he became intimately acquainted with the joys of freedom, leading him toward serious consideration of escape. In his autobiographical writings, Douglass was reluctant, for fear of possible repercussions, to name the friends who had aided in his escape. However, one of his written statements that "I owe much to the society of these young men," is perhaps an oblique reference to their efforts to encourage and assist him in obtaining freedom, the greatest benefit he received from membership in the East Baltimore Mental Improvement Society.[28]

The debating club sponsored social activities as well and it was at one such affair that Douglass met Caroline County, Maryland native, Anna Murray. She was the eighth of twelve children and the first to be born free to Bambarra and Mary Murray. At seventeen she arrived in Baltimore and found employment as a domestic with a Fells Point family. It is possible she also worked as a cook; the Mary Murray who operated a small restaurant in Fells Point may have been Anna's mother. Barely literate, Anna was a loyal and devoted friend, encouraging Douglass to study the violin and helping him to purchase music books. Anna was also deeply involved in Douglass's escape plans, making the sailor suit he wore as a disguise and selling her personal belongings in order to provide funds, to supplement Douglass's savings, for the journey. A week after his safe arrival in New York, Anna followed and they were married by the Rev. James W. C. Pennington, another Marylander who had escaped slavery. Five years older than Douglass, Anna encouraged and nurtured her husband and, during his frequent absences, supported and sustained the family throughout their forty-four-year marriage.

Using the abolitionist movement as a springboard, Frederick Douglass became an orator, journalist, recruiter for the Union Army, ambassador and public servant. He was, above all and in all of his activities, a humanitarian, which Webster's New Collegiate Dictionary defines as a person promoting human welfare and social reform. He fought vehemently against discrimination and inequality in all arenas. An advocate of temperance, Douglass was also an early proponent of universal—he used the word to include females—suffrage. He was opposed to charitable activities which relegated recipients to a subordinate, impotent position. He believed that Christians should adhere to those tenets of their faith which governed human interaction. While supportive of Blacks' efforts toward self-improvement and inclusion in American society, he idealistically hoped for a society in which opportunity would be influenced by neither race nor gender.

Douglass returned to Baltimore on many occasions, usually in an effort to assist Blacks in some uplifting activity. In August 1865, he was present for the dedication of the Douglass Institute. For twenty-five years the Institute was the cultural, political and educational center of the Black community. Located on Lexington Street near Monument Street, the building was owned by whites. A group of Black men rented it and used it to provide space for concerts, lectures, meetings and the production of a newspaper.

Douglass lectured at the Centennial Methodist Church in May 1879 in an effort to help the church secure funds with which to prevent foreclosure. In his speech, "The Conditions and Relations of the

Colored People", he recalled the conditions under which he had lived in Fells Point, delineated the positive changes which had occurred since that time and encouraged the congregation to believe that continued progress was possible. After his death, the church installed a stained-glass window in the wall behind the pulpit in his memory.

Echoing his speech at Centennial, Douglass delivered a similar message at Bethel A.M.E. Church in December 1879 when he spoke in support of the effort to hire Black teachers in Black public schools. Douglass was warmly received and interrupted several times by applause, particularly when he made reference to the desire of Blacks, not for special treatment, but for equality of treatment.

Accompanied by his daughter and son, Douglass attended the funeral of his friend, John W. Locks, in 1884. During his final visit to Baltimore on 22 June 1894, he took great pride in addressing the audience at the sixth annual commencement exercises of the Colored High School.[29] The school was renamed in his honor in 1923.[30] In a less pleasant vein, Douglass attempted, in 1864, to visit the widowed Sophia Auld. He was angrily rebuffed by her son, Benjamin, who found Douglass's autobiographical portrayal of his mother to be unjust and unflattering. Racism may have once again reared its ugly head as Benjamin may have misinterpreted Douglass's writings; he appears to have attempted to present a balanced and objective discussion of his relationship with Sophia Auld. Douglass seemed also to have been more favorably disposed to Sophia than to her husband, Hugh.

During his 1864 visit to Baltimore, Douglass was unexpectedly reunited with his sister Eliza who, having learned of his planned lectures, came to visit from Talbot County. They had been separated since his 1838 departure from St. Michael's. Approximately two years older than Douglass, Eliza remained a slave of Thomas Auld until she was sold for one hundred dollars to Peter Mitchell, a free Black man whom she subsequently married. An illiterate woman, Eliza worked for many years as a domestic earning five dollars a month. Her husband, a farm laborer, probably earned less than fifteen dollars monthly. With a family of nine children, the Mitchells must have struggled for many years to pay their debt to Auld. Most of Eliza's children, as limited educationally as their parents, were also employed as farm laborers and domestics. They lived in a repressive environment where whites prevented them from purchasing land and responded violently to their efforts to achieve economic independence and parity.

Eliza can be considered a successful woman if one considers the hard work and determination necessary to obtain freedom. Unlike her brother, she had not been able to radically alter her circumstances or to provide her children with the opportunity to do the same. Her family background and early influences were similar to her brother's. Since she was approximately two years older than Douglass, it is conceivable that she had greater opportunities to bond with their mother. What Eliza did not have was an opportunity to become literate. Additionally, she lacked exposure to an atmosphere which fostered the hope of freedom. Eliza did not, on a regular basis, have the opportunity to observe and interact with groups of Black people who had either gained their freedom or who had never been enslaved.

What was missing from Eliza's life was the opportunity to hear, on a regular basis, a gospel of liberation. She experienced a society in which the survival and comfort of one group was dependent on the labor and discomfort of another. The difference between Eliza Bailey and Frederick Douglass was that Eliza never lived in Baltimore. The attitudes and ideologies to which Douglass subscribed and which directed his activities were developed and nurtured during his Baltimore years. The self-confidence, spirit of hope and skills he acquired during his Baltimore years enabled him to rise to the position of leadership from which he labored in the cause of social reform.

ENDNOTES

1. National Park Service, *Thoughts For All Time* (Washington, D.C.: National Park Service, 1992), 20.
2. Ibid., 23.
3. Frederick Douglass, *Narrative of the Life of Frederick Douglass* (New York: Penguin Books, Inc., 1968). Chapter ten contains a vivid description of the treatment of slaves deemed to be rebellious.
4. Dickson J. Preston, *Young Frederick Douglass, The Maryland Years.* (Baltimore: The Johns Hopkins University Press, 1980), 87.
5. Bettye Gardner, "Ante-Bellum Black Education in Baltimore," *Maryland Historical Magazine* 71 (Fall 1976): 361.
6. Oral tradition among the descendants of John W. Locks, an African American friend of Douglass, holds that Locks provided reading lessons to Douglass.
7. Bettye C. Thomas, "A Nineteenth Century Black Operated Shipyard, 1866-1884: Reflections Upon Its Inception and Ownership," *The Journal of Negro History* 49 (January 1974): 2.
8. Christopher Phillips, *Freedom's Port, The African American Community of Baltimore, 1790–1860* (Urbana: University of Illinois Press, 1997), 111.
9. Phillips, 159.
10. William B. McClain, *Black People in the Methodist Church, Whither Thou Goest?* (Nashville: Abingdon Press, 1984), 56.
11. Phillips, 24.
12. Barbara Jeanne Fields, *Slavery and Freedom on the Middle Ground* (New Haven: Yale University Press, 1985), 62.
13. Phillips, 94.
14. Gardner, 360.
15. Suzanne Ellery Greene Chapelle and others. *Maryland, A History of Its People* (Baltimore: The Johns Hopkins University Press, 1986), 129.
16. Phillips, 163.
17. Gardner, 363.
18. Norman G. Rukert, *The Fells Point Story* (Baltimore: Bodine and Associates, 1976), 37.
19. Gardner, 366.
20. Phillips, 165.
21. There is variance in scholarly opinion as to which church(s) Douglass belonged to. He appears on the membership rolls of Sharp Street. Membership rolls for Centennial-Caroline are no longer extant and as of this writing, records of Bethel have not been examined.
22. For a detailed outcome of the results of the debates see Christopher Phillips, "The Dear Name of Home: Resistance to Colonization in Antebellum Baltimore," *Maryland Historical Magazine* 91 (Summer 1996): 181–202.
23. Phillips, 169.
24. George F. Bragg, Jr. *Men of Maryland* (Baltimore: Church Advocate Press, 1925).
25. See *The Baltimore Sun*, 11 March 1884 and *The Cleveland Gazette*, 22 March 1884.
26. *Two Hundredth Anniversary Program*, Centennial-Caroline United Methodist Church, 1973.
27. Preston, 149.
28. McFeely, 68.
29. Bragg, 60.
30. *Baltimore Afro-American*, 10 September 1983.

Donna T. Hollie, PhD, is a charter member of the Agnes Kane Callum (Baltimore) chapter of AAHGS and serves as vice president for history. A retired professor of history, her publications include *African Americans of Fauquier County Virginia* and *Through The Tax Assessor's Eyes: Enslaved People, Free Blacks and Slaveholders in Early Nineteenth Century Baltimore*. Hollie has contributed articles to AAHGS's newsletter and journal, *Encyclopedia Virginiana*, *Black Women in America* and Henry Louis Gates's *The African American National Biography*.

Roots: Tracing the Family History of James McCune and Malvina Barnett Smith, 1783–1937, Part 1

ABSTRACT

Dr. James McCune Smith (1813–1865) was a pioneering African American physician, intellectual, author, and polymath. Though widely forgotten for over a century, McCune Smith's outsize contributions to African American history are gaining more recognition in scholarship and public memory. However, few details are known about the personal history of McCune Smith and his family, a lack which can only serve to impoverish scholarly and public understanding of McCune Smith and his legacy. This article presents newly discovered information and explores tantalizing clues about McCune Smith's family history. In doing so, it hopes to outline a helpful methodology for others conducting genealogical research into African American families. Additionally, this article explores how race and identity affected the experiences and opportunities of McCune Smith and his extended family which, in turn, may have contributed to knowledge of McCune Smith's life and legacy becoming largely lost to his descendants and to history.

KEYWORDS
James McCune Smith, African American history, genealogy, race, identity, passing, New York history

Introduction

Dr. James McCune Smith (1813–1865) was the first known African American to practice medicine with a medical degree; authored the first case report by an African American physician delivered to a medical association; was the first known African American to have work published in medical journals; and was an early adopter of applying sophisticated statistical analysis in his medical, scientific, and abolitionist writings. He was a formative member of the African American press and a leader in New York educational, voting rights, and political abolitionist activism. He was also the first African American author of experimental literature (as argued by Judith Mulcahy and by Henry Louis Gates, Jr. in his forward to The *Works of James McCune Smith*, ed. John Stauffer); is widely recognized among his contemporary African American community as a premier intellectual and professional figure; and can fairly be described as the first full-fledged African American polymath.

After over a century of relative obscurity—an obscurity difficult to explain given his outsize role in African American history—McCune Smith is gaining more recognition in scholarship and public memory. However, few details are known about the personal history of McCune Smith and his family, a lack which can only serve to impoverish scholarly and public understanding of this pioneering and influential figure. This article seeks to correct this deficiency by presenting newly discovered information and exploring tantalizing clues about McCune Smith's family history.

In describing the research process presented herein, this article also seeks to describe a helpful methodology for others who wish to conduct African American genealogical research, following such scholars as Heather Andre Williams. Williams has described various and creative means by which African Americans have historically sought lost knowledge of family members and ancestors during and after the era of slavery. Inspired by Williams' and others' work, this article will explore McCune Smith's early family history; that of his wife Malvina and her Barnett family; and of the family McCune Smith and Malvina made together. It will also include some anecdotes which evoke their personalities and circumstances. As Charles L. Blockson writes in Black Genealogy, "simply discovering the names of your ancestors isn't enough . . . You want to find out how they lived and really get a feel for the world and the society they inhabited." The article will explore this family history in three sections: McCune Smith's Early Family History; The Barnett Family; and Family of James McCune and Malvina Barnett Smith.

In doing so, this article also seeks to illustrate how the largely lost history of the Smith and Barnett families represents a double loss. First, this article reveals many possibilities and limitations inherent in tracing genealogies often obscured by the dehumanizing institution of slavery and the United States racial caste system that arose from it. Secondly, this article seeks to show how race and identity affected the experiences and opportunities of individuals within the Smith and Barnett families and how these, in turn, contributed to knowledge of their forebears becoming largely lost to history. McCune Smith's rejection from institutions of higher learning in his native New York State on account of race, and James Parker Barnett's ejection, for the same reason, from New York University's College of Physicians and Surgeons, are two examples of the ways race and racial discrimination impacted these connected families. Hardships associated with identification as "African" within the United States' racial caste system appear to have influenced the changing racial identities of both families through the years. As we shall see, issues of race and identity and their associated hardships culminate in difficult choices faced, and made, by latter generations of the Barnett and Smith families. These, in turn, may have helped to obscure McCune Smith's legacy as a preeminent African American intellectual and activist.

McCune Smith's Early Family History

James McCune Smith's mother Lavinia Smith was born about 1783 in South Carolina. This is known from her name, family status, age, and place of birth recorded in the 1850 and 1860 federal and 1855 New York state censuses when she was a member

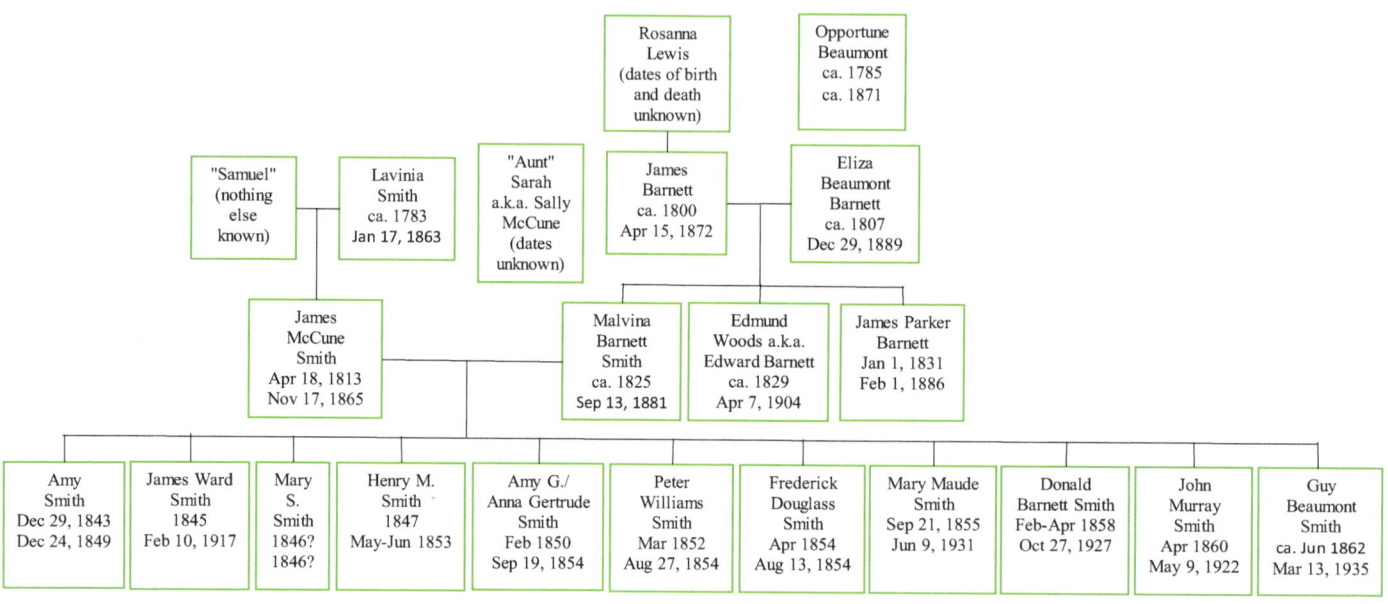

Family tree chart: Amy M. Cools, 2020

of her son James and daughter-in-law Malvina's household. Public records of Lavinia for her years in South Carolina have not yet been located; hints about her early life are currently limited to tidbits among others' descriptions. For example, in his obituary for McCune Smith, friend and colleague Robert Hamilton tells us that 'His mother [Lavinia] was from Charleston, S.C., whence she came when a young girl, leaving behind a large circle of relations.' Even her only known son, McCune Smith, wrote rarely of Lavinia; he was generally reticent to offer personal details about his family to the public, with some exceptions pertaining to his writings on race and racism.

In one 1844 instance, McCune Smith wrote of his family's origins: "I beg to say that, being the son of a slave, owing my liberty to the emancipation act of the State of New-York, and having kindred in a southern State, some of them slaveholders, others slaves...." Since, as McCune Smith stated in 1851, his father was "a descendant of the Puritans, a real Caucasian," Lavinia would have been his only enslaved parent. She was, McCune Smith added, of mixed race, a "mulatto." There is one extant anecdote featuring Lavinia from her pre-New York years, offered by McCune Smith to illustrate the pervasiveness of the United States racial caste system. Lavinia told her son of a man "in her home, Charleston, S.C.," who offered a $10 reward if a white man helped him to capture his runaway horse, and $5 if a black man would do so.

Details about McCune Smith's father are even more nebulous; only two primary sources provide a name. Both are among McCune Smith's student records at the University of Glasgow, Scotland, where he received his bachelor's, master's, and medical degrees in 1835, 1836, and 1837, respectively. These records provide only a first name, Samuel, and one adds a few details in Latin: "Filius natu maximus Samuelis, Mercatoris apud New York" ("Eldest natural son of Samuel, merchant in New York"). As we have seen, McCune Smith later identified Samuel as white. While scholars often surmise that Samuel was also his mother's legal owner, there is no confirmation of this in the historical record. It is also likely that McCune Smith never met his father; possible that he knew nothing of him besides his name, race, and profession; and possibly, not even these. In a letter to Frederick Douglass as editor of the Frederick Douglass' Paper (FDP) in 1852, McCune Smith indicated that he shared the experience of Douglass, who knew nothing of his own father. "We of doubtful parentage ... cannot look anywhere in particular for 'forefathers' day' and 'fatherland' ..." Meticulous research has thus far failed to yield any records of a Samuel Smith that fit the few parameters considered above, indicating that the name "Samuel" may possibly have been entered into McCune Smith's university records for convenience or respectability's sake. The search for Lavinia in New York only deepened the mystery.

Details about Lavinia's life only appear in public records following her arrival in the North. The 1855 New York state census indicates that Lavinia arrived in New York City around 1805. Author Craig D. Townsend refers to her fleetingly: "Lavenia [sic] Smith was brought to New York City ... by her owner," citing the 1855 New York census and a note in the papers of Rhoda Golden Freeman. However, this statement is in tension with McCune Smith's description of Lavinia as "self-emancipated." Maritcha Lyons, McCune Smith's goddaughter, recalled in her 1929 unpublished memoir "Memories of Yesterdays" that though she did not know when Lavinia arrived in New York City, she was a "slave who had been given her freedom to make her eligible to testify in a court of justice." Lyons did not provide a context for this special dispensation. In any case, Lavinia's legal status as a free woman would been assured when New York's emancipation act went into full effect on 4 July 1827.

Lavinia Smith does not appear in any records of New York inhabitants for relevant years until 1811 and 1812, when Longworth's American Almanac, New-York Register, and City Directory lists her as "Smith, widow Lavinia, tailor" at 1 Hester St., corner of Norfolk. This was located in the notoriously dense lower-working-class neighborhood of Five

Points, also home to a sizable, close-knit African American community. Intriguingly, this Lavinia is described as a widow well before McCune Smith's birth in 1813. While it is possible that at least some of these entries refer to another Lavinia Smith, there are no multiple listings for that or similar names in the New York City directories during those years. Compelling circumstantial evidence, which we shall consider, also indicates that the only listed Lavinia Smith refers to McCune Smith's mother. If so, this would further indicate that "Samuel" may not have been a Smith since a husband surnamed Smith had already died; that "Samuel" may not have been married to Lavinia; or that "Samuel" may have been a placeholder name for an unknown father.

Lavinia Smith disappears from the city directories until at least 1815; *Longworth's* for that year lists a "Smith, widow Lavina"—note the variant name spelling—at "203 Division." She disappears again to re-emerge in *Longworth's* for 1820 and 1822, where she is listed as living at "44 Orange." That was also the address of the New York African Society for Mutual Relief, a beneficial society founded in 1808. As member and abolitionist John Jay Zuille wrote in his *Historical Sketch*, the Society acquired the property in August of 1820 and "erected a building which was used for its meetings and to accommodate other societies. It was in line with the residences of many of its prominent members." (McCune Smith would become a member in 1841). By this time, Orange St. was among those in the Five Points—a neighborhood previously notorious for its swampy streets, dilapidated buildings, and epidemics of yellow fever—that had been revitalized and built over with large wood-frame buildings run by absentee landlords. Edwin G. Burrows and Mike Wallace describe these as "de facto boardinghouses for the wage-laborers now settling the area."

It is here that we can look to Philip A. Bell, whose reminisces of McCune Smith and his family provide more rare glimpses into their origins. Bell was a lifelong friend of McCune Smith's who, Bell put it, "knew him as none but his wife and lamented mother knew him." In 1873, Bell wrote a three-part series on New York City's Underground Railroad for his paper *The Elevator*. In one instalment, Bell recalled an incident in which McCune Smith's mother "Lavenia Smith"—again, note the variant name spelling—and his aunt "Mrs. Sally McCune" assisted in delivering one Margaret Green from slavery. Bell described how Lavinia and Sally—both from Charleston—brought Green to Bell's family home seeking shelter for her in the fall of 1816. They were afraid that since Green's legal owners knew Lavinia and Sally, they would seek for her at their home.

This opened an intriguing line of research: if she was living in New York City in 1816, Sally McCune might be listed in city directories, even sharing an address with Lavinia. Sure enough, a search for "Sally" or "Sarah"—the proper name for the diminutive "Sally"—McCune turned up an entry in *Mercein's City Directory* for 1820, at 44 Orange. As we have seen, this was also Lavinia's address that year. Sarah McCune is listed as a teacher. *Longworth's* for 1820 also lists a "M'Cune, widow Sarah" at 44 Orange St. Subsequent searches for Sally or Sarah McCune failed to turn up anything in New York City directories until *Doggett's New-York City Directory, for 1846 and 1847*. It lists a "M'Cune, Sarah, widow of James." While this discovery appeared to suggest an inspiration for both McCune Smith's first *and* middle names, cross-referencing in previous directories revealed that this Sarah was the widow of another James McCune who had died in 1838, well after McCune Smith's aunt was first listed as a widow. Nevertheless, the last name of McCune Smith's Aunt Sally does suggest the inspiration for his middle name. "Sarah McCune" otherwise disappears from the historical record following the 1820 issue of *Mercein's* and Bell's account.

Given the known relationships between McCune Smith, Lavinia Smith, and Sarah McCune, and the apparent lack of involvement of Samuel in their lives—making it less likely that Sarah was among McCune Smith's paternal relations—there is a strong possibility that Sarah and Lavinia were sisters. This makes tracing their origins more difficult. Given that Lavinia and Sarah first appear in the historical record as widows, there is no indication of the last name they would have shared. Research in digitized census and slavery records for South Carolina—through genealogical sites such as Ancestry.com, FamilySearch.org, AfriGeneas.com, LowcountryAfricana.com, and more—on this supposition has thus far failed to turn up records identifying Lavinia and Sarah in the same household, with or without last names included, between 1783–1805. This, though disappointing, is unsurprising: such records for enslaved and free African Americans are relatively rare. Research is ongoing.

As another example, there are two Lavinias listed in the *New York Slavery Records Index* (https://nyslavery.commons.gc.cuny.edu/birth-registrations-and-abandonments/).

Lavinia Smith, widow, reappears in New York City directories in 1825 at 25 Norfolk and in 1827 at 20 Norfolk, where she is listed as a "tailoress." By this time, McCune Smith was well established at the African Free School on Mulberry St., also in Five Points, where he excelled. For example, he was regularly selected to participate in advanced classes. At fourteen years old, he was also chosen to direct classes for two months while its instructor, Charles Andrews, was absent due to illness. Hamilton wrote that Lavinia raised McCune Smith alone and supported both of them with the work of "her own hands," which "with the grace of God this means was ever ample and abundant." However, Lavinia's profession may not have generated enough income to provide herself and her son with both a nurturing home and a full education, at least, not to the satisfaction of their mutually supportive community. As we shall see, they received support from multiple quarters.

For one, Bell recalled that McCune Smith's "first tuition was received from 'Grandma Weaver.'" Again, Bell's account suggested an intriguing line of inquiry. If there was a woman named Weaver associated with the Smith family, it was possible she would be found in New York City directories at an address within the Smiths' community. Sure enough, *Longworth's* lists a "Weaver Mrs. 44 Orange" in 1821, within the period during which McCune Smith began attending the African Free School. This, as we have seen, was the same address given for Lavinia in 1820 and 1822, and for Sarah in 1820. *Longworth's* for 1822 also lists a "Weaver widow Mary" at 137 Collect St., also in Five Points. This was also near St. Philip's Episcopal Church, McCune Smith's parish throughout his life.

Censuses, directories, and other contemporary sources, however, fail further to identify a Mrs., a Mary, or any female Weaver in New York City except for records of an 1820's parishioner of nearby Allen Street Methodist Episcopal Church. These sources, however, do not identify her age, race, or other details. "Grandma Weaver" may have been a grandmotherly figure to McCune Smith, or she may have been his actual grandmother. Searches based on the latter supposition have also failed to yield results. All that the historical record currently confirms from Bell's account is that a woman named Weaver was indeed connected to McCune Smith's family. She is mentioned nowhere else in relevant historical documents.

The next directory listing for Lavinia Smith, in 1829's *Longworth's* at 33 Centre St., provides further insight into another source of support for the Smith family. This was also the address of St. Philip's, where the Rev. Peter Williams, Jr. served as pastor and where McCune Smith would later serve as vestryman and treasurer. As the scholarship describes, Williams was a mentor to McCune Smith and a key figure in his pursuit of higher education. He was among those who guided McCune Smith in his independent studies after graduating from the African Free School; helped McCune Smith apply to colleges and universities; and obtained tuition funds for him to attend the University of Glasgow after New York institutions rejected McCune Smith's applications on account of race. Lavinia's address at 33 Centre St. further indicates that the Smith and Williams connection extended beyond the relationship of student and mentor. Lyons appears to have confirmed this larger family connection when she wrote "It may be referred that the family with which his mother was connected was his patron."

Lavinia's address at St. Philip's indicates not only that deeper connection between the Smith and Williams families, but that she served the parish in some capacity as well. It is also possible, even likely, that her son did not live with her there then, but rather with the Williams family. The 1830 federal census reveals that the four persons in Peter and Sarah Williams' household included a male between the ages of 10 and 23—McCune Smith was seventeen at the time—and the Williams had no son of their own. Given Peter Williams' leading role in facilitating McCune Smith's education, this would have been a convenient living arrangement.

To further fill in the picture of the relationship between the Smith and Williams families, we first return to Bell. In 1865, Bell recalled that Peter Williams was McCune Smith's "guardian" who initially encouraged McCune Smith to study for the ministry. Williams' guardianship of McCune Smith was likely an informal one: Williams' will and probate documents do not describe him as McCune Smith's legal guardian, or McCune Smith as his ward. The intimate and enduring relationship between the Smith and Williams families, however, is otherwise well attested. For example, McCune Smith described sending two letters to his mother and five to Williams in his 1832 travel journal written *en route* to Glasgow; Williams visited McCune Smith while he was in Britain and traveled with him to Europe; McCune Smith named one of his sons for Williams; he wrote a biographical account of Williams after his death; and Williams' widow Sarah made her home with the James McCune and Malvina Smith family, along with Lavinia, for at least a decade and a half of the later years of her life. Lavinia Smith died at the Smith family home on 17 January 1863 following a year-long decline in her health. She was eighty years old.

(continued on page 53)

ENDNOTES

1. James McCune Smith and John Stauffer, *The Works of James McCune Smith: Black Intellectual and Abolitionist* (Oxford: Oxford University Press, 2006), xiii–xv; Leslie A. Falk, "Black Abolitionist Doctors and Healers, 1810–1885," *Bulletin of the History of Medicine* 54, no. 2 (1980): 260; Thomas M. Morgan, "The Education and Medical Practice of Dr. James McCune Smith (1813–1865), First Black American to Hold a Medical Degree," *Journal of the National Medical Association* 95, no. 7 (July, 2003): 603, 604, 608, 610–11; Heidi L. Lujan and Stephen E. DiCarlo, "First African-American to Hold a Medical Degree: Brief History of James McCune Smith, Abolitionist, Educator, and Physician," *Advances in Physiology Education* 43, no. 2 (April 1, 2019): 134–36.

2. Irvine Garland Penn, *The Afro-American Press and Its Editors* (Springfield: Willey & Co., 1891), 33–34, 40, 98; Rhoda Golden Freeman, "The Free Negro in New York City in the Era Before the Civil War" (New York, Columbia University, 1966), 145–47, 153, 352–53, ProQuest Dissertations and Theses; McCune Smith and Stauffer, *Works of James McCune Smith*, x–xi, xiii, xxiii–xxviii, xxxii–xxxiii; Judith Mulcahy, "James McCune Smith: The Communipaw Connection," *Nineteenth-Century Prose* 34, no. 1–2 (2007): 360, 362–63; "Reception of Dr. Smith," The Colored American (TCA), October 28, 1837; Frederick Douglass, "Dr. James McCune Smith—Among the Colored Men of Note in This Country . . . ," *Frederick Douglass' Paper* (FDP), June 3, 1853; William Wells Brown, *The Black Man: His Antecedents, His Genius, and His Achievements* (Boston: James Redpath, 1863), 205–6.

3. Heather Andrea Williams, *Help Me to Find My People: The African American Search for Family Lost in Slavery* (Chapel Hill: University of North Carolina Press, 2012), 11–12, 14–16, 123, 141–42, 147–68, 197–200.

4. Charles L. Blockson, *Black Genealogy* (Baltimore: Black Classic Press, 1991), 15.

5. On the use of names: James McCune Smith, following James Stauffer and many other scholars, is referred to by the compound last name McCune Smith, rather than Smith, to avoid confusion with friend, frequent correspondent, and abolitionist Gerrit Smith. The other elder James discussed in this article, James Barnett, will be generally referred to by the last name Barnett. The younger son of James Barnett and the elder son of

James McCune Smith will be referred to by their first and middle names, James Parker and James Ward, to avoid confusion with the elder Jameses. The married women of the family will be referred to by first names since they changed their last names during their lifetime, for consistency's sake and to avoid confusion with other members of the family who share their last names. Members of the family following elder generations, with the exception of McCune Smith, will be introduced in paragraphs by first and middle names to distinguish them as members of latter generations, and to show how their names often paid tribute to ancestors and to important figures in the families' lives.

6 1850 United States Census, New York, New York County, New York, digital image s.v. "James McCune Smith," FamilySearch.org; 1855 New York State Census, for James McCune Smith, New York, New York County, digital image s.v. "James McCune Smith," *FamilySearch.org*; 1860 United States Census, New York, New York County, New York, digital image s.v. "Jas. M. Smith," FamilySearch.org.

7 Robert Hamilton, "Dr. James McCune Smith," *The Anglo-African*, December 9, 1865.

8 James McCune Smith, "Freedom and Slavery for Africans," *New-York Daily Tribune*, January 20, 1844; "The Poughkeepsie Slave Case," *The Liberator*, September 12, 1851; James McCune Smith, "From Our New York Correspondent," *FDP*, December 15, 1854.

9 *Nomina Magistrorum Artium Universitatis Glasguensis AB Anno 1763–1888*, 181, 184; University of Glasgow, University Prizes, 26, 38; *Nomina Medicinae Doctorum Universitatis Glasguensis AB Anno 1769–1888*, 68–69; University of Glasgow, *University Register: Medicine 1822–23 to 1842–43*, 84; *A Roll of the Graduates of the University of Glasgow: from 31st December, 1727 to 31st December, 1897*, 56.

10 For example, Craig D. Townsend and Heidi L. Lujan and Stephen E. DiCarlo make this claim. See Townsend, *Faith in Their Own Color: Black Episcopalians in Antebellum New York City* (New York: Columbia University Press, 2005), 74; Lujan and DiCarlo, "First African-American to Hold a Medical Degree," 134.

11 James McCune Smith, "Letter from Communipaw [4 Feb 1852]," *FDP*, February 12, 1852.

12 1855 New York State Census, "James McCune Smith." There is a record of a 'Black Slave Lavinia' (no last name or age recorded) giving birth to a son in New York in 1802. While it is possible this may refer to our Lavinia, the year predates the year given in the 1855 census for Lavinia's arrival in NYC. See Henrietta Anderson, "[Birth Certificate of Francis Jones, a Male Black Child]," New-York Historical Society (digital), May 13, 1802. https://cdm16694.contentdm.oclc.org/digital/collection/p15052coll5/id/24323.

13 Townsend, *Faith in Their Own Color: Black Episcopalians in Antebellum New York City*, 74. Freeman authored the first comprehensive study of free African Americans in New York before the Civil War.

14 Title VII, original note to § 16, *Revised Statutes of the State of New York, As Altered by the Legislature, including the Statutory Provisions of a General Nature, Passed from 1828 to 1835 Inclusive*, Volume III (Albany: Packard And Van Benthuyasen, 1836), 554; Maritcha Remond Lyons. "Memories of Yesterdays: All of Which I Saw and Part of Which I Was—An Autobiography" (unpublished manuscript, 1929), 77, Schomburg Center for Research in Black Culture, New York Public Library; Leslie M. Harris, *In the Shadow of Slavery: African Americans in New York City, 1626–1863* (Chicago: University of Chicago Press, 2003), 73.

15 David Longworth, *Longworth's American Almanac, New-York Register, and City Directory* (New York: David Longworth, 1811), 272; David Longworth, *Longworth's American Almanac, New-York Register, and City Directory* (New York: David Longworth, 1812), 290; Edwin G. Burrows and Mike Wallace, *Gotham: A History of New York City To 1898* (New York: Oxford University Press, 1998), 400, 479; Carla L. Peterson, *Black Gotham: A Family History of African Americans in Nineteenth-Century New York City* (New Haven: Yale University Press, 2011), 63–64.

16 Stauffer also suggests that "Samuel" may have been a fictional or placeholder name; see McCune Smith, *Works*, xix.

17 Longworth, *Longworth's*, 1820, 54; John Jay Zuille, *Historical Sketch of the New York African Society for Mutual Relief* (New York: New York African Society for Mutual Relief, 1892), 4–5, 16, 31.

18 David Longworth, *Longworth's American Almanac, New-York Register, and City Directory* (New York: David Longworth, 1815), 386; Thomas Longworth, *Longworth's American Almanac, New-York Register, and City Directory* (New York: Thomas Longworth, 1820), 406; Thomas Longworth, *Longworth's American Almanac, New-York*

19. Philip A. Bell, "Death of Dr. Jas. McCune Smith," *The Elevator*, December 22, 1865; Philip A. Bell, "Underground Railroad in New York: No. 1." *The Elevator*, January 18, 1873.
20. William A. Mercein, *Mercein's City Directory, New-York Register, and Almanac* (New York: William A Mercein, 1820), 294; Longworth, *Longworth's*, 1822, 296; John Doggett, *Doggett's New-York City Directory, for 1846 and 1847* (New York: John Doggett, Jr., 1846), 250.
21. There may be a connection between Sarah McCune and the slaveowning McKewn family of Charleston, SC; records of enslaved people connected to the family for relevant years have not yet been located. See "U.S. Wills and Probate Records, 1670–1980, Charleston, South Carolina, USA," digital image s.v. "Will of Archibald McKewn, [d.] abt. 1829," *Ancestry.com*; "U.S. Wills and Probate Records, 1670–1980, Charleston, South Carolina, USA," digital Image s.v. "[Probate Document for] Mary McKewn, [d.] abt. 1847," *Ancestry.com*; Fold3, "Slaves in the Estate of Mary McKewn, Oak Hill Plantation, Charleston, 1853," https://www.fold3.com/page/282787495-slaves-in-the-estate-of-mary-mckewn-oak-hill-plantation-charleston-1853.
22. Thomas Longworth, *Longworth's American Almanac, New-York Register, and City Directory* (New York: Thomas Longworth, 1825), 393; Thomas Longworth, *Longworth's American Almanac, New-York Register, and City Directory* (New York: Thomas Longworth, 1827), 448; Charles C. Andrews, "A Dialogue: Spoken by Jas. M. Smith and William Hill at a Public Exam in 1822. Written for the Occasion by C.C.A Teacher," in "Addresses and Pieces Spoken at Examinations, 1818–1826" (unpublished manuscript), 45–50; Charles C. Andrews, *The History of the New-York African Free-Schools: From Their Establishment in 1787, to the Present Time* (New York: Mahlon Day, 1830), 61; New-York African Free-School, "New-York African Free School Records, 1817–1832" (New York, 1832), 101, 103–10, 116, 118, New-York Historical Society, https://cdm16694.contentdm.oclc.org/digital/collection/p15052coll5/id/28365; Morgan, "Education," 605–6.T
23. Hamilton, "Dr. James McCune Smith."
24. Bell, "Death of Dr. Jas. McCune Smith;" Thomas Longworth, *Longworth's American Almanac, New-York Register, and City Directory* (New York: Thomas Longworth, 1821), 458; Longworth, *Longworth's*, 1822, 466; John H. Hewitt, *Protest and Progress: New York's First Black Episcopal Church Fights Racism* (New York/London: Garland Publishing, 2000), 62–70, 90, 122; 127.
25. "A List of Probationers in the Methodist Episcopal Church in the City of New York 1822–1832," digital image s.v. "Mary Weaver," *Ancestry.com*; "Methodist Episcopal Church Classes 1825," digital image s.v. "Mary Weaver," *Ancestry.com*; Methodist Episcopal Church, New York City, "Methodist Episcopal Church Classes 1826: Classes in Allen Street," digital image s.v. "Mary Weaver, *Ancestry.com*; "A Register of the Names of the Members of the Methodist Episcopal Church in the City of New York, 1822–1831," digital image s.v. "Mary Weaver," *Ancestry.com*; "Methodist Episcopal Church Classes 1829," digital image s.v. "Mary Weaver," *Ancestry.com*.
26. Thomas Longworth, *Longworth's American Almanac, New-York Register, and City Directory* (New York: Thomas Longworth, 1829), 520; Thomas Longworth, *Longworth's American Almanac, New-York Register, and City Directory* (New York: Thomas Longworth, 1828), 651; C. Peter Ripley, *The Black Abolitionist Papers*. Vol. I: The British Isles, 1830–1865 (Chapel Hill: University of North Carolina Press, 1991), 58 n.9; McCune Smith and Stauffer, *Works of James McCune Smith*, xx; Peterson, *Black Gotham*, 115; Lujan and DiCarlo, "First African-American to Hold a Medical Degree," 135; Lyons, "Memories of Yesterdays," 77.
27. Longworth, *Longworth's*, 1829, 612; Thomas Longworth, *Longworth's American Almanac, New-York Register, and City Directory* (New York: Thomas Longworth, 1830), 641; 1830 United States Census, New York, New York County, New York, digital image s.v. "Peter Williams," *Ancestry.com*.
28. Bell, "Death of Dr. Jas. McCune Smith;" "New York, Wills and Probate Records, 1659–1999," digital image s.v. "Peter Williams" (probate date November 20, 1840), *Ancestry.com*; "New York, Wills and Probate Records, 1659-1999," digital image s.v. "Peter Williams" (Petition of Sarah Williams), *Ancestry.com*.
29. "Dr. Smith's Journal [Liverpool, 13-15 Sep 1832]," *TCA*, March 16, 1839; Martin R. Delany, "Died," *FDP*, October 6, 1854; James McCune Smith, "Memoir of Peter Williams (Fragment)," in *The Colored Patriots of the American Revolution, With Sketches of Several Distinguished Colored Persons: To Which Is Added a Brief Survey of the Condition and*

Prospects of Colored Americans (Boston: Robert F. Wallcut, 1855), 321–23; 1855 New York State Census, New York, New York County, digital image s.v. "James McCune Smith;" 1860 United States Census, New York, New York County, New York, digital image s.v. "Jas. M. Smith;" Bell, "Death of Dr. Jas. McCune Smith;" 1865 New York State Census, New York, New York County, digital image s.v. "James M. Smith," *FamilySearch.org*.

30 "Death of an Aged Lady," *The Anglo-African*, January 24, 1863.

BIBLIOGRAPHY

1830 United States Census, New York, New York County, New York, digital image s.v. "Peter Williams." *Ancestry.com*.

1850 United States Census, New York, New York County, New York, digital image s.v. "James McCune Smith." *FamilySearch.org*.

1855 New York State Census, New York, New York County, digital image s.v. "James McCune Smith." *FamilySearch.org*.

1860 United States Census, New York, New York County, New York, digital image s.v. "Jas. M. Smith." *FamilySearch.org*.

1865 New York State Census, New York, New York County, digital image s.v. "James M. Smith." *FamilySearch.org*.

A Roll of the Graduates of the University of Glasgow: From 31st December, 1727 to 31st December, 1897. Glasgow: James Maclehose & Sons, 1898.

Anderson, Henrietta. "[Birth Certificate of Francis Jones, a Male Black Child]." New-York Historical Society (digital), May 13, 1802. https://cdm16694.contentdm.oclc.org/digital/collection/p15052coll5/id/24323.

Andrews, Charles C. "A Dialogue: Spoken by Jas. M. Smith and William Hill at a Public Exam in 1822. Written for the Occasion by C.C.A Teacher." In *Addresses and Pieces Spoken at Examinations, 1818–1826*, 45–50. New York: New-York African Free School, 1818. https://cdm16694.contentdm.oclc.org/digital/collection/p15052coll5/id/28491.

———. *The History of the New-York African Free-Schools: From Their Establishment in 1787, to the Present Time*. New York: Mahlon Day, 1830.

Bell, Philip A. "Death of Dr. Jas. McCune Smith." *The Elevator*. December 22, 1865.

———. "Underground Railroad in New York: No. 1." *The Elevator*. January 18, 1873.

Blockson, Charles L. *Black Genealogy*. Baltimore: Black Classic Press, 1991.

Burrows, Edwin G., and Mike Wallace. *Gotham: A History of New York City To 1898*. New York: Oxford University Press, 1998.

"Death of an Aged Lady." *The Anglo-African*, January 24, 1863.

Delany, Martin R. "Died." *Frederick Douglass' Paper*. October 6, 1854.

Doggett, John. *Doggett's New-York City Directory, for 1846 and 1847*. New York: John Doggett, Jr., 1846.

Douglass, Frederick. "Dr. James McCune Smith." *Frederick Douglass' Paper*. June 3, 1853.

Falk, Leslie A. "Black Abolitionist Doctors and Healers, 1810–1885." *Bulletin of the History of Medicine* 54, no. 2 (1980): 258–72.

Freeman, Rhoda Golden. "The Free Negro in New York City in the Era Before the Civil War." Columbia University, 1966. ProQuest Dissertations and Theses.

Hamilton, Robert. "Dr. James McCune Smith." *The Anglo-African*, December 9, 1865.

Harris, Leslie M. *In the Shadow of Slavery: African Americans in New York City, 1626–1863*. Chicago: University of Chicago Press, 2003.

Hewitt, John H. *Protest and Progress: New York's First Black Episcopal Church Fights Racism*. New York/London: Garland Publishing, 2000.

Longworth, David. *Longworth's American Almanac, New-York Register, and City Directory*. New York: David Longworth, 1811.

———. *Longworth's American Almanac, New-York Register, and City Directory*. New York: David Longworth, 1812.

———. *Longworth's American Almanac, New-York Register, and City Directory*. New York: David Longworth, 1815.

Longworth, Thomas. *Longworth's American Almanac, New-York Register, and City Directory*. New York: Thomas Longworth, 1820.

———. *Longworth's American Almanac, New-York Register, and City Directory*. New York: Thomas Longworth, 1821.

———. *Longworth's American Almanac, New-York Register, and City Directory*. New York: Thomas Longworth, 1822.

———. *Longworth's American Almanac, New-York Register, and City Directory*. New York: Thomas Longworth, 1825.

———. *Longworth's American Almanac, New-York Register, and City Directory*. New York: Thomas Longworth, 1827.

———. *Longworth's American Almanac, New-York Register, and City Directory*. New York: Thomas Longworth, 1828.

———. *Longworth's American Almanac, New-York Register, and City Directory*. New York: Thomas Longworth, 1829.

———. *Longworth's American Almanac, New-York Register, and City Directory*. New York: Thomas Longworth, 1830.

Lujan, Heidi L., and Stephen E. DiCarlo. "First African-American to Hold a Medical Degree: Brief History of James McCune Smith, Abolitionist, Educator, and

Physician." *Advances in Physiology Education* 43, no. 2 (April 1, 2019): 134–39.

Lyons, Maritcha Remond. "Memories of Yesterdays: All of Which I Saw and Part of Which I Was—An Autobiography." New York, NY, 1929. Williamson Family Papers, Maritcha Remond Lyons, Writings, 1869–1917. Schomburg Center for Research in Black Culture, New York Public Library.

McCune Smith, James. "Dr. Smith's Journal [Liverpool, 13–15 Sep 1832]." *The Colored American*. March 16, 1839.

———. "Freedom and Slavery for Africans." *New-York Daily Tribune*. January 20, 1844.

———. "From Our New York Correspondent [1, 8, and 9 Dec 1854]." *Frederick Douglass' Paper*. December 15, 1854.

———. "Letter from Communipaw [4 Feb 1852]." *Frederick Douglass' Paper*. February 12, 1852.

———. "Memoir of Peter Williams (Fragment)." In *The Colored Patriots of the American Revolution, With Sketches of Several Distinguished Colored Persons: To Which Is Added a Brief Survey of the Condition and Prospects of Colored Americans*, 321–23. Boston, MA: Robert F. Wallcut, 1855.

McCune Smith, James, and John Stauffer. *The Works of James McCune Smith: Black Intellectual and Abolitionist*. Oxford: Oxford University Press, 2006.

Mercein, William A. *Mercein's City Directory, New-York Register, and Almanac*. New York: William A. Mercein, 1820.

"Methodist Episcopal Church Classes 1825," digital image s.v. "Mary Weaver." Ancestry.com.

"Methodist Episcopal Church Classes 1826: Classes in Allen Street," digital image s.v. "Mary Weaver." Ancestry.com.

"Methodist Episcopal Church Classes 1829," digital image s.v. "Mary Weaver." Ancestry.com.

Morgan, Thomas M. "The Education and Medical Practice of Dr. James McCune Smith (1813–1865), First Black American to Hold a Medical Degree." *Journal of the National Medical Association* 95, no. 7 (July 2003): 603–14.

Mulcahy, Judith. "James McCune Smith: The Communipaw Connection." *Nineteenth-Century Prose* 34, no. 1–2 (2007): 359–68.

"New York, Wills and Probate Records, 1659-1999," digital image s.v. "Peter Williams" (petition of Sarah Williams). Ancestry.com.

"New York, Wills and Probate Records, 1659–1999," digital image s.v. "Peter Williams" (probate date November 20, 1840). Ancestry.com.

New-York African Free-School. "New-York African Free School Records, 1817–1832." New York, NY, 1832. New-York Historical Society. https://cdm16694.contentdm.oclc.org/digital/collection/p15052coll5/id/28365.

Nomina Magistrorum Artium Universitatis Glasguensis AB Anno 1763–1888. Glasgow: University of Glasgow, 1763.

Nomina Medicinae Doctorum Universitatis Glasguensis AB Anno 1769–1888. Glasgow: University of Glasgow, 1769.

Penn, Irvine Garland. *The Afro-American Press and Its Editors*. Springfield: Willey & Co., 1891.

Peterson, Carla L. *Black Gotham: A Family History of African Americans in Nineteenth-Century New York City*. New Haven: Yale University Press, 2011.

"Reception of Dr. Smith." *The Colored American*. October 28, 1837.

Ripley, C. Peter. *The Black Abolitionist Papers*. Vol. I: The British Isles, 1830–1865. Chapel Hill: University of North Carolina Press, 1991.

Fold3. "Slaves in the Estate of Mary McKewn, Oak Hill Plantation, Charleston, 1853." https://www.fold3.com/page/282787495-slaves-in-the-estate-of-mary-mckewn-oak-hill-plantation-charleston-1853.

"The Poughkeepsie Slave Case." *The Liberator*. September 12, 1851.

"A Register of the Names of the Members of the Methodist Episcopal Church in the City of New York, 1822–1831," digital image s.v. "Mary Weaver." Ancestry.com.

Revised Statutes of the State of New York, As Altered By The Legislature, including the Statutory Provisions of a General Nature, Passed from 1828 to 1835 Inclusive, Volume III. Albany: Packard And Van Benthuyasen, 1836.

Townsend, Craig D. *Faith in Their Own Color: Black Episcopalians in Antebellum New York City*. New York: Columbia University Press, 2005.

University of Glasgow. *University Prizes*. Glasgow: University of Glasgow, 1834.

———. *University Register: Medicine 1822–23 to 1842–43*. Glasgow: James Maclehose & Sons, 1843.

"U.S. Wills and Probate Records, 1670–1980, Charleston, South Carolina, USA," digital image s.v. "[Probate Document for] Mary McKewn, [d.] abt. 1847." Ancestry.com.

"U.S. Wills and Probate Records, 1670–1980, Charleston, South Carolina, USA," digital image s.v. "Will of Archibald McKewn, [d.] abt. 1829," Ancestry.com.

Wells Brown, William. *The Black Man: His Antecedents, His Genius, and His Achievements*. Boston: James Redpath, 1863.

Williams, Heather Andrea. *Help Me to Find My People: The African American Search for Family Lost in Slavery*. Chapel Hill: University of North Carolina Press, 2012.

Zuille, John Jay. *Historical Sketch of the New York African Society for Mutual Relief*. New York: New York African Society for Mutual Relief, 1892.

Roots: Tracing the Family History of James McCune and Malvina Barnett Smith, 1783–1937, Part 2

The Barnett Family

The historical record reveals few details about Malvina Barnett's family prior to her father James Barnett's emergence in New York City directories in the late 1820s. However, this article can introduce two members to the scholarship: Malvina's grandmothers. Malvina's maternal grandmother Opportune Beaumont is listed in 1850, 1855, and 1870 censuses among the Barnett family household. They indicate that Opportune was born in Guadeloupe, West Indies about 1785; that she was "mulatto;" and that she could not read or write. Her daughter Eliza's father has not been located in the historical record. Other than a web page for her burial at Cypress Hills Cemetery in 1871, Opportune disappears from the historical record.

Malvina's paternal grandmother is named in her son's will, for which his son-in-law James McCune Smith was designated an executor. Written two decades before Barnett's death, the 1851 will left his mother "Rosanna Lewis, should she survive me, such support and comfortable living out of my estate either by paying her board or otherwise." The beneficiaries of Barnett's estate were also instructed to give whoever lived with Rosanna at the time of her death $100 to pay for funereal and associated expenses. Since Rosanna was a Lewis rather than a Barnett in 1851, she was likely unmarried when Barnett was born about 1800, or subsequently remarried to a man surnamed Lewis. Since the will does not refer to Barnett's father, he was likely no longer living or involved with the family.

Since no other family documents have been found for Rosanna, we turn to public records. Censuses record two women named Rosanna Lewis in New York State of an age to be Barnett's mother. One is listed in the 1830 and 1840 federal censuses, living in New York City's 10th and 14th ward, respectively. In each case, "Rosanah"/"Rosanna" was designated head of household—indicating she was unmarried or widowed—of a "free colored" family. The change in the number of adult male household members of James's approximate age—one between the ages of 36–53 no longer appears in the 1840 census—might be consistent with his departure by the time it was taken if the census taker mistakenly recorded James in that older age category in 1830. Another Rosanna Lewis, age 68 and born in New York, appears in the 1850 federal census as the wife of James Lewis, age 69, living in Newstead, Erie County, New York. Neither Rosanna has been located elsewhere in censuses. However, New York City directories contain entries which could refer to our Rosanna. One, a "Rosannah Lewis," is listed only once before the 1850s, at 44 Delancey St. in 1829. A "Rosanna Lewis" is also listed as a milliner in the late 1850s through the mid-1860s. The milliner Rosanna, however, is a less likely candidate. If she were old enough to be Barnett's mother, she would have been at an advanced age to be working, especially since her son was then well-to-do enough to support her.

James Barnett's wife Eliza Beaumont first appears in the historical record in the 1850 federal census. Here, the Barnett and Smith families become easier to trace; it is the first census to record full names and ages for all members of households. It reveals that Eliza and Barnett were married and living in Williamsburgh—later part of Brooklyn—with their sons James Parker and Edmund Woods and Eliza's mother Opportune. Their eldest child, Malvina, had married and left the household by then. The 1850 and subsequent censuses reveal that Eliza was born about 1807 in New York City and that she could read, but not write. While she was designated "mulatto" or "of color" in earlier censuses, by 1870 she was not designated by race. By 1880, she and her children were designated as "white." The historical record has not revealed a marriage date for James Barnett and Eliza Beaumont. The year of birth of Malvina—their first child—in about 1825 suggests they were already married. Eliza would have been quite young, still in her teens, at the time of her marriage, as her only daughter would be at the time of her own.

James Barnett had established his lifelong career as a tinsmith by 1828, when he is first listed as such in *Longworth's New York City Directory* at 140 Maiden Lane. By then, Maiden Ln. was among New York City streets connected to a new centralized gasworks which illuminated streets, businesses, and homes; perhaps the shop's access to the gasworks contributed to its success and longevity. In the late 1820s, the Barnetts lived at 64 Frankfort St; in 1830, they moved to Duane St. The family grew to include Edmund Woods, born about 1829, and James Parker, born January 1, 1831. 1840s New York City directories list both the Barnett home and shop at 140 Maiden Ln. Presumably, the family had moved into the multi-use building.

By 1840, the Barnett family had the means to send their first child to college: Malvina was enrolled in the Rutgers Female Institute that year. In 1841, she continued her studies there, advancing "during the first term of the third academic year." Established in 1838, Rutgers was little more than a mile east of the family home. Malvina's studies in Rutgers' First Academic Department included Abercrombie's *Classical Literature*, Karnes' *Elements of Criticism*, Paley's *Natural Theology and Evidences of Christianity*, maths and sciences, grammar, rhetoric, composition, logic, bookkeeping, and Latin and "Biblical Archaeology and Ecclesiastical History." While Rutgers was deemed both controversial and progressive for providing a comprehensive liberal arts and scientific education for women and girls, the historical record is silent regarding its racial composition. Given that New York's educational institutions were still racially segregated—as McCune Smith discovered when his college applications were rejected in the early 1830s—it is likely Rutgers assumed Malvina to be white and that she and her family did not disabuse them of that perception. Malvina did well at Rutgers, winning a Gold Composition Medal in 1841. Although historian Arturo Alfonso Schomburg states that Malvina graduated from Rutgers, this appears to be incorrect. Malvina is listed among enrolled students in 1841, but not among the Institute's graduates in that or subsequent years. Her academic career was likely cut short by her early marriage.

In 1844, James Parker also commenced his higher education. He first attended New York University (NYU) that academic year, joining one of the university's literary societies and earning academic prizes. He earned his bachelor's and master's degrees there in 1848 and 1851, respectively. While at NYU, James Parker trained under an "eminent practicing physician" who introduced him to NYU's College of Physicians and Surgeons (CPS). This physician, apparently, was Dr. C. E. Pierson, who was listed as his preceptor in the *Annual Catalogue of the College of Physicians and Surgeons* for the academic year 1849–1850.

In October 1850, James Parker was revealed to the trustees of CPS to have nonwhite ancestry, though this apparently had gone unobserved—as it had for Malvina at Rutgers—by faculty and students when he began attending classes at the medical school. The historical record does not reveal how or why this revelation was made. Upon that discovery, James Parker was promptly expelled. Barnett, on behalf of his son, took the trustees of the CPS to court in 1851. The case, *Barnett v. the Trustees of the College of Physicians and Surgeons*, ended up in the New York State Supreme Court before Justice James J. Roosevelt. The trustees of the CPS argued "that by the course and usage" of the medical school, "persons of color are not candidates for the degree of Doctor of Medicine, nor has that degree, or the attendance on the lectures of the professors, ever been of right granted to any person of color." They argued further that James Parker's continuing attendance "would prevent . . . numerous students from attending its instruction" and thereby "would be injurious to the usefulness of the college." Representing the Barnetts, John Jay II—whose father was president of the African Free School when McCune Smith attended—argued that since Barnett was a landowner "entitled to the full rights and privileges of citizenship" and that his son met the academic qualifications, the latter should have the right to attend NYU. The case remained undecided when New York newspapers stopped reporting on the case after the spring of 1853; the court record had not been located.

James Parker's ambition to become a physician may have been delayed by the CPS trustees, but not for long. He continued to practice medicine in 1853–1854: McCune Smith's reports as attending physician for the Colored Orphan Asylum record James Parker's services there as assistant physician. James Parker was also admitted to the medical school at Dartmouth College in 1853, where he obtained his medical degree in 1854. In 1863, McCune Smith again enlisted James Parker's help at the Colored Orphan Asylum. When it was looted and burned in the 1863 New York City Draft riots, James Parker was serving as attending physician while McCune Smith was ill. As the Asylum's co-founder and secretary Anna Shotwell wrote, "The Physician in attendance, Dr. Barnett, had through the day of the mob felt great anxiety as to the safety of the Institution. He was carefully watching, and gave the first alarm." The children, fortunately, all survived the attack.

While the 1855 New York State census identifies all members of the Barnett family as "mulatto," the 1870 federal census—the next census they have been located in—assigns a racial classification to Opporture only. Her entry's race box is filled by an unspecific "X" rather than the specific indicators "W," "B," "M," "C," or "I" often recorded under the descriptors "White," "Black," "Mulatto," "Chinese," or "Indian" provided in the census heading. This may indicate that the nonwhite ancestry of other members of the Barnett family was not apparent to the census taker. According to the US Department of Commerce's *Negro Population 1790–1915*, racial classification was assigned according to census takers' judgments, not self-identification. In 1850, federal census takers "were instructed simply in enumerating colored persons to write 'B' or 'M' in the space on the schedule, . . . leaving the space blank in the case of whites." Subsequent censuses did not include this instruction. Perhaps some census takers—such as the one who recorded the Barnett family in 1870—continued that earlier practice of only recording perceived nonwhite ancestry. The Barnetts' physical appearance may help explain why the historical record remains silent on other hardships the Barnett family may have endured on account of race besides James Parker's discrimination case.

Throughout the 1850s and 1860s, James Barnett continued to accumulate property and personal wealth. His 1851 will left cash, property, and investments to Eliza until the time of her death except for "all the stock in trade and the tools and implements and fixtures belonging or appertaining to my business of Tin Smith or to the shop" to their second son Edmund Woods "providing that he shall continue to be employed or remain in the said business." By 1870, Barnett had retired, and he died on April 15, 1872. Eliza outlived her husband by over sixteen years, dying on December 29, 1888 in Newark, New Jersey. She was likely living with her grandson James Ward Smith—who had settled there—at the time of her death. By the time she made her will in 1886, Eliza was a widow of means, indicating her prudent management of the substantial legacy Barnett had left her. In turn, she bequeathed to her surviving child Edmund and to most of her many grandchildren substantial personal property and cash bequests as well as the use of the family plot in Brooklyn's Cypress Hills Cemetery.

Edmund Woods did follow in his father's footsteps as a tinsmith. Though the 1850 census does not record his trade, it is evident that the 22-year-old was already well established in his father's business by then. As we have seen, Barnett's 1851 will left it to Edmund so long as he kept it going. However, the 1855 New York state census reveals a time of multiple transitions in Edmund Woods' life soon after. It also reveals a possible explanation for why Edmund seemed to disappear from the historical record for nearly three decades. Searches for Edmund following the 1855 census initially turned up nothing until he reappeared in his brother's 1883 will. A city directory for 1871, however, provided a key detail for filling in that gap.

It turns out that Edmund Woods appears not once, but twice, in the 1855 census. In an entry recorded on June 13, 1855, Edmund—misspelled "Edmon"—appears as a 26-year-old "mulatto," unmarried tinsmith, a lifelong resident of New York City living in his parents' household. In another entry recorded in Brooklyn on June 20th, he appears as "Edward Barnet," age twenty-nine, tinsmith, and fifteen-year resident of Brooklyn, living with wife Margreth Barnett, age 26, and two daughters: Lidia Ann Barnet, age 11, born in New York County, and Sarah Barnett, age 1 month, born in Kings County. No race is recorded for the family. The second census entry was discovered following a new line of research opened up by the chance notice of an entry in Trow's directory for 1871. Above James Barnett's entry for his tinsmith's shop at 140 Maiden Ln. is one for an Edward Barnett, also listed as a tinsmith at the same address. His place of residence is listed as Brooklyn. Edward is also listed under that name, once with his middle initial "W," in 1872 and 1873 at that Maiden Ln. shop address.

It is left to explain why Edmund/Edward Barnett is listed in two separate households under two different names in the 1855 census. One explanation is suggested by his status as unmarried in the first census entry and married in the next; the presence of a new daughter; and the apparent absence of a marriage record for Edmund/Edward and Margreth: they may not have been legally married in 1855. Another could be Edmund's desire to create a new identity with a new family, a new name, a new hometown, and a new racial identity to increase opportunities in a racially discriminatory society. In any case, there is no evidence that this partially double life created rifts within the Barnett family. Edmund/Edward continued in business with his father until the latter retired about 1870. His mother and brother included him—still referring to him as Edmund—and his children in their wills. James Parker's 1883 will left money to Edmund's children equally with Malvina's, as did Eliza's. Eliza's 1886 will also designated Edmund as executor—while providing us with his middle name. James Parker's will also names Edmund's children, serving as cross-references for census entries for his family under his new name.

Subsequent searches for "Edward Barnett" revealed a wealth of information, starting with the 1860 federal census. This census lists him only as Edward (this article will hereafter refer to him by his chosen name) living in Williamsburgh with "Margaret," daughters Sarah and Elizabeth, and son Edward. The 1865 New York state census reveals that 35-year-old Margreth was married once before Edward and was the mother of 11 children upon the birth of another son, James. Lidia had left the household, perhaps to live with her father's family. Elizabeth, who had been an infant at the time of the previous census, was not listed, nor was she named in James Parker's will. Presumably, then, she did not survive childhood. Edward and Margreth continued to live in Williamsburg; by 1880, the children had left home—even 17-year-old James—and Edward and Margreth were living alone. They would have at least one more son, John, also named in James Parker's will. Sarah, Edward, James, and John would survive their parents.

In 1862, city directories began to list Edward as an artisan in his own right. Directories and censuses would continue to list his occupation variously as smith, tinsmith, and plumber through 1880. Edward continued in the business his father had left him until late in life. He died a widower on April 7, 1904, at age 75, and was buried in the family plot in Cypress Hills. According to Edward's obituary, which refers to him by his original name, he had been a long-time volunteer firefighter, at one time president of the local firefighter's association.

Though Edward's younger brother James Parker continued to practice medicine until at least 1881, he had also become a pharmacist by 1861 (perhaps inspired by his brother-in-law McCune Smith). In subsequent years he is listed variously in censuses and directories as a physician, chemist, manufacturing chemist, and "color" or paint manufacturer through 1884. James was also involved in several real estate transactions on his own and with his widowed sister Malvina in the 1870s. He remained single, usually living with his parents—and after his father's death in 1872, his mother—until, at age 47, he married Helen A. Foster on January 24, 1878. James's family were listed without racial identifiers or identified as white in state and federal censuses after 1855. A little over one year after their marriage, James and Helen's first child, Seymour F., was born. They had three more children: Doré W., Gladys, and Leroy. James was financially successful: he left Helen, his children, and his nieces and nephews substantial bequests of cash, personal goods, and property when he died on February 1, 1886. His death left Helen a widow and a mother of four. James was buried in the family plot in Cypress Hills, where Helen would be buried when she died about 34 years later.

(continued on page 63)

ENDNOTES

1. See "Tracing the Family History" Part One, for the family tree accompanying this article series.
2. 1850 United States Census, Williamsburg, Kings County, New York, digital image s.v. "Jas. P. Barnet," *Ancestry.com*; 1855 New York State Census, New York, New York County, digital image s.v. "James Barnett," *Ancestry.com*; 1870 United States Census, New York, New York County, digital image s.v. "James Barnett," *Ancestry.com*; "Opportune Beaumont (1786-1871)," Find a Grave, accessed April 29, 2017, https://www.findagrave.com/memorial/144539786/opportune-beaumont
3. "New York Wills and Probate Records, 1659-1999," digital image s.v. "James Barnett" (probate date July 7, 1850), *Ancestry.com*.
4. 1830 United States Census, New York, New York County, New York, digital image s.v. "Rosanah Lewis" (Ward 10), *Ancestry.com*; 1840 United States Census, New York, New York County, New York, digital image s.v. "Rosanna Lewis," *Ancestry.com*; 1850 United States Census, Newstead, Erie County, New York, digital image s.v. "Rosanna Lewis," *Ancestry.com*; Thomas Longworth, *Longworth's American Almanac, New-York Register, and City Directory* (New York: Thomas Longworth, 1829), 353; Henry Wilson and John F. Trow, *Trow's New-York City Directory* (New York: John F. Trow, 1857), 491; Wilsom and Trow, *Trow's*, 1860, 508; Wilson and Trow, *Trow's*, 1862, 515; Wilson and Trow, *Trow's*, 1864, 523.
5. 1850 United States Census, "Jas. P. Barnet;" 1855 New York State Census, "James Barnett;" 1870 United States Census, "James Barnett;" 1875 New York State Census, Brooklyn, Kings County, digital image s.v. "Eliza Barnett," *Ancestry.com*; 1880 United States Census, Brooklyn, Kings County, New York, digital image s.v. "Eliza Barnet," *Ancestry.com*; 1850 United States Census, New York, New York County, New York, digital image s.v. "James McCune Smith," *FamilySearch.org*.
6. 1850 United States Census, "Jas. P. Barnet;" Longworth, *Longworth's*, 1828, 110; Edwin G. Burrows and Mike Wallace, *Gotham: A History of New York City To 1898* (New York: Oxford University Press, 1998), 439.
7. Longworth, *Longworth's*, 1828, 110; Longworth, *Longworth's*, 1829, 77; Longworth, *Longworth's*, 1830, 116.
8. 1850 United States Census, "Jas. P. Barnet;" 1860 United States Census, Williamsburg, Kings County, New York, digital image s.v. "Edward Barnett," *Ancestry.com*; 1860 United State Census, New York, New York County, New York, digital image s.v. "James P. Barnett," *Ancestry.com*; "Edward Barnett (1829–1904)," Find a Grave, accessed April 4, 2020, https://www.findagrave.com/memorial/167432660/edward-barnett; "Dr James Parker Barnett (1831–1886)," Find a Grave, accessed April 13, 2020, https://www.findagrave.com/memorial/119761559/james-parker-barnett. Edmund's given age is

inconsistent in census entries, and no source has yet been found which provides his birthdate.

9 John Doggett, *The New-York City Directory, for 1844 & 1845* (New York, NY: John Doggett, 1844), 28; Doggett, *New-York City Directory*, 1845, 29. An 1851 street directory indicates that 140 Maiden Lane housed persons and businesses; see Doggett, *Doggett's*, 1851, 255.

10 'Rutgers Female Institute', *The New World* 1, no. 10 (8 August 1840); Rutgers Female Institute, *Third Annual Circular of the Rutgers Female Institute* (New York, NY: Rutgers Female Institute, 1841), 11; Burrows and Wallace, *Gotham*, 799; Rutgers Female Institute, *Third Annual Circular*, 3, 4–5; Rutgers Female Institute, 3–10; "A Veteran Teacher's Life," *Times Union*, May 16, 1888; "Dr. West's Life," *The Standard Union*, January 14, 1893; Rhoda Golden Freeman, "The Free Negro in New York City in the Era Before the Civil War" (Columbia University, 1966), 99, 334, 347, 362, 366–69, ProQuest Dissertations and Theses; Arturo Alfonso Schomburg, "Dr. James McCune Smith," *Negro History Bulletin* 9, no. 2 (November 1, 1945), 42.

11 News accounts of an 1853 New York Supreme Court case involving James Parker Barnett, his father James Barnett, and the New York College of Physicians and Surgeons at NYU over the latter's ejection of James Parker from classes once they discovered his African ancestry, provide some details of J.P. Barnett's career at NYU, as well as James Barnett's status as a landowner in 1853. See "Denial of a Diploma to a Colored Student," *Buffalo Morning Express and Illustrated Buffalo Express*, May 2, 1853" and "Supreme Court—Special Term. Before Hon. Judge Roosevelt: A Curious Colored Case," *New York Daily Herald*, April 21, 1853.

12 University of the City of New-York, *A Catalogue of the Officers and Alumni of the University of the City of New-York* (New York: University of the City of New-York, 1852), 16; General Alumni Society, *General Alumni Catalogue of New York University 1833–1906* (New York: General Alumni Society, 1906), 29; "Denial of a Diploma;" Dartmouth College, *Catalogue of the Faculty and Students of Dartmouth College, for the Academical Year 1853–4* (Hanover: Dartmouth College, 1853), 5.

13 "Supreme Court;" "James J. Roosevelt [from The Judges of the New York Court of Appeals: A Biographical History, Ed. Hon. Albert M. Rosenblatt, 2007]," Historical Society of the New York Courts, accessed May 9, 2020, https://history.nycourts.gov/figure/james-roosevelt/; "Denial of a Diploma;" Charles C. Andrews, *The History of the New-York African Free-Schools: From Their Establishment in 1787, to the Present Time* (New York: Mahlon Day, 1830), 51; John H. Hewitt, *Protest and Progress: New York's First Black Episcopal Church Fights Racism* (New York/London: Garland Publishing, 2000), 60, 65–66, 69–71.

14 *Seventeenth Annual Report of the Association for the Benefit of Colored Orphans.* (New York: Association for the Benefit of Colored Orphans, 1853), 14–16; *Eighteenth Annual Report of the Association for the Benefit of Colored Orphans* (New York: John F. Trow, 1854), 20–22; Dartmouth College, *Catalogue of the Faculty and Students*, 7; Dartmouth College, *Catalogue Senatus Academici et Eorum Qui Munera et Officia Academica Gesserunt Quique Alicujus Fradus Laurae Donati Sunt, in Collegio Dartmuthensi, Hanoverae, in Republica Neo-Hantoniensi* (New York: Dartmouth College, 1858), 65; *Twenty-Seventh Annual Report*, 12, 17; Leslie M. Harris, *In the Shadow of Slavery: African Americans in New York City, 1626–1863* (Chicago: University of Chicago Press, 2003), 280–86.

15 1855 New York State Census, "James Barnett;" 1870 United States Census, "James Barnett;" *Negro Population 1790–1915* (Washington, D.C.: United States Department of Commerce, Bureau of the Census, 1918), 207–8.

16 1855 New York State Census, "James Barnett;" *New-York Tribune* and Barnett, "To Let—Two Neat Two-Story, Attic and Basement Houses," *New-York Tribune*, May 10, 1856; "Wills and Probate," "James Barnett;" 1870 United States Federal Census, "James Barnett;" "New York, New York, Extracted Death Index, 1862–1948," s.v. "James Barnett," *Ancestry.com*.

17 "New York, Wills and Probate Records, 1659–1999," digital image s.v. "Eliza Barnett" (probate date February 18, 1889), *Ancestry.com*. This document, signed by her son and executor of her will, Edmund W. Barnett, indicates that she was living in Newark 'on account of her health,' and gives a Newark address for James Ward Smith.

18 1850 United States Census, "Jas. P. Barnet;" "Wills and Probate," "James Barnett;" "New York, Wills and Probate Records, 1659–1999," digital image s.v. "James P. Barnett," (probate date June 2, 1883), *Ancestry.com*.

19 1855 New York State Census, "James Barnett;" 1855 New York State Census, Brooklyn, Kings County, digital

image s.v. "Edward Barnet," *Ancestry.com*; Wilson and Trow, *Trow's*, 1871, 64; Wilson and Trow, *Trow's*, 1872, 65; Wilson and Trow, *Trow's*, 1873, 69.

20 "Wills and Probate," "James P. Barnett;" "Wills and Probate," "Eliza Barnett."

21 1860 United States Census, "Edward Barnett;" 1865 New York State Census, Brooklyn, Kings County, New York, digital image s.v. "Edward Barnett," *Ancestry.com*; "Wills and Probate," "James P. Barnett;" 1870 United States Census, Williamsburg, Kings County, New York, digital image s.v. "Edward Barnett," *Ancestry.com*; 1875 New York State Census, Brooklyn, Kings County, digital image s.v. "Edward Barnett," *Ancestry.com*; 1880 United States Census, Brooklyn, Kings County, New York, digital image s.v. "Edward Barnett," *Ancestry.com*; "Edmund W. Barnett [Obituary], *The Brooklyn Citizen*, April 11, 1904.

22 J. Lain, *Brooklyn City Directory* (Brooklyn: J. Lain & Co., 1862), 17; Lain, *Brooklyn City Directory* (Brooklyn, 1866, 22; George T. Lain, *Brooklyn City and Business Directory* (Brooklyn: Lain & Co., 1868), 25; Lain, *Brooklyn City Directory*, 29; Wilson and Trow, *Trow's*, 1874, 66; Wilson and Trow, *Trow's*, 1875, 66; Wilson and Trow, *Trow's*, 1876, 67; Lain, *Brooklyn City Directory*, 1876, 35; Lain, *Brooklyn City Directory*, 1877, 34; Lain, *Brooklyn City Directory*, 1878, 34; Lain, *Brooklyn City Directory*, 38; Lain, *Brooklyn City Directory*, 1880, 40.

23 "New York, New York, Index to Death Certificates, 1862–1948," s.v. "Edward Barnett," (died April 7, 1904), *Ancestry.com*; "Edmund W. Barnett [Obituary]."

24 Lain, *Brooklyn City Directory*, 1881, 41; Wilson and Trow, *Trow's*, 1861, 54.

25 Wilson and Trow, *Trow's*, 1862, 54; Wilson and Trow, *Trow's*, 1866, 61; Wilson and Trow, *Trow's*, 1867, 61; Wilson and Trow, *Trow's*, 1868, 63; Wilson and Trow, *Trow's*, 1869, 63; Wilson and Trow, *Trow's*, 1870, 67; 1870 United States Census, "James Barnett;" Wilson and Trow, *Trow's*, 1871, 64; Wilson and Trow, *Trow's*, 1873, 69; Lain, *Brooklyn City Directory*, 1874, 31; Lain, *Brooklyn City Directory*, 1875, 34; Wilson and Trow, *Trow's*, 1875, 66; Lain, *Lain's*, 1876, 35; Lain, *Lain's*, 1878, 38; Lain, *Lain's*, 1879, 38; Lain, *Lain's*, 1880, 40; 1880 United States Census, Brooklyn, Kings County, New York, digital image s.v. "Jas. P. Barnett," *Ancestry.com*; Lain, *Lain's*, 1881, 41; Lain, *Brooklyn City Directory*, 1882, 43; Lain, *Brooklyn City Directory*, 1884), 49.

26 "Real Estate Transfers [from Malvina Smith to James P. Barnett]," *The Brooklyn Daily Eagle*, June 6, 1873; "Legal Notices: County Court, Kings County," *The Brooklyn Daily Eagle*, August 16, 1877; "Real Estate Transfers [from James P. Barnett]," *Times Union*, November 13, 1879.

27 1875 New York State Census, "James Barnett" (son); "New York, Marriage Newspaper Extracts, 1801-1880 (Barber Collection)," digital image s.v. "Dr James P Barnett," (publication date January 25, 1878), *Ancestry.com*, 1–14, 1963–66:28.

28 1880 United States Census, "Jas. P. Barnett;" "Wills and Probate," "Eliza Barnett;" "Dr James Parker Barnett (1831–1886)."

REFERENCES

1830 United States Census, New York, New York County, New York, digital image s.v. "Rosanah Lewis" (Ward 10). *Ancestry.com*.

1840 United States Census, New York, New York County, New York, digital image s.v. "Rosanna Lewis." *Ancestry.com*.

1850 United States Census, New York, New York County, New York, digital image s.v. "James McCune Smith." *Family Search.org*.

1850 United States Census, Williamsburg, Kings County, New York, digital image s.v. "Jas. P. Barnet." *Ancestry.com*.

1850 United States Census, Newstead, Erie County, New York, digital image s.v. "Rosanna Lewis." *Ancestry.com*.

1855 New York State Census, Brooklyn, Kings County, digital image s.v. "Edward Barnet." *Ancestry.com*.

1855 New York State Census, New York, New York County, digital image s.v. "James Barnett." *Ancestry.com*.

1860 United States Census, Williamsburg, Kings County, New York, digital image s.v. "Edward Barnett." *Ancestry.com*.

1860 United State Census, New York, New York County, New York, digital image s.v. "James P. Barnett." *Ancestry.com*.

1865 New York State Census, Brooklyn, Kings County, digital image s.v. "Edward Barnet." *Ancestry.com*.

1870 United States Census, Williamsburg, Kings County, New York, digital image s.v. "Edward Barnett." *Ancestry.com*.

1870 United States Census, New York, New York County, digital image s.v. "James Barnett." *Ancestry.com*.

1875 New York State Census, Brooklyn, Kings County, digital image s.v. "Edward Barnet." *Ancestry.com*.

1875 New York State Census, Brooklyn, Kings County, digital image s.v. "Eliza Barnett." *Ancestry.com*.

1875 New York State Census, Brooklyn, Kings County, digital image s.v. "James Barnett" (son). *Ancestry.com*

1880 United States Census, Brooklyn, Kings County, New York, digital image s.v. "Edward Barnett." *Ancestry.com*.

1880 United States Census, Brooklyn, Kings County, New York, digital image s.v. "Eliza Barnet." *Ancestry.com*.

1880 United States Census, Brooklyn, Kings County, New York, digital image s.v. "Jas. P. Barnett." *Ancestry.com*.

"A Veteran Teacher's Life: The Career of Prof. Benjamin West as an Educator." Times Union. May 16, 1888.

Andrews, Charles C. *The History of the New-York African Free-Schools: From Their Establishment in 1787, to the Present Time.* New York: Mahlon Day, 1830.

Burrows, Edwin G., and Mike Wallace. *Gotham: A History of New York City To 1898.* New York: Oxford University Press, 1998.

College of Physicians and Surgeons. *Annual Catalogue of the College of Physicians and Surgeons in the City of New York, University of the City of New-York.* New York: College of Physicians and Surgeons, 1850.

Dartmouth College. *Catalogue of the Faculty and Students of Dartmouth College, for the Academical Year 1853–4.* Hanover: Dartmouth College, 1853.

———. *Catalogue Senatus Academici et Eorum Qui Munera et Officia Academica Gesserunt Quique Alicujus Fradus Laurea Donati Sunt, in Collegio Dartmuthensi, Hanoverae, in Republica Neo-Hantoniensi.* New York: Dartmouth College, 1858.

"Denial of a Diploma to a Colored Student." *Buffalo Morning Express and Illustrated Buffalo Express.* May 2, 1853.

Doggett, John. *Doggett's New York City Street Directory, for 1851.* New York: John Doggett, Jr., 1851.

———. *The New-York City Directory, for 1844 & 1845.* New York: John Doggett, 1844.

———. *The New-York City Directory, for 1845 & 1846.* New York: John Doggett, 1845.

Find a Grave. "Dr James Parker Barnett (1831–1886)." Accessed 13 April 13, 2020. https://www.findagrave.com/memorial/119761559/james-parker-barnett.

"Dr. West's Life: Fifty Years Devoted to the Furthering of Female Education." *The Standard Union.* January 14, 1893.

"Edmund W. Barnett [Obituary]." *The Brooklyn Citizen.* April 11, 1904.

Eighteenth Annual Report of the Association for the Benefit of Colored Orphans. New York: John F. Trow, 1854.

Find a Grave. "Edward Barnett (1829–1904)." Accessed April 9, 2020. https://www.findagrave.com/memorial/167432660/edward-barnett.

Find a Grave. "Opportune Beaumont (1786–1871)." Accessed April 29, 2020. https://www.findagrave.com/memorial/144539786/opportune-beaumont.

Freeman, Rhoda Golden. "The Free Negro in New York City in the Era Before the Civil War." Columbia University, 1966. ProQuest Dissertations and Theses.

General Alumni Society. *General Alumni Catalogue of New York University 1833–1906.* New York: General Alumni Society, 1906.

Harris, Leslie M. *In the Shadow of Slavery: African Americans in New York City, 1626–1863.* Chicago: University of Chicago Press, 2003.

Hewitt, John H. *Protest and Progress: New York's First Black Episcopal Church Fights Racism.* New York/London: Garland Publishing, 2000.

Historical Society of the New York Courts. "James J. Roosevelt [from The Judges of the New York Court of Appeals: A Biographical History, Ed. Hon. Albert M. Rosenblatt, 2007]." Accessed May 9, 2020. https://history.nycourts.gov/figure/james-roosevelt/.

Lain, George T. *Brooklyn City and Business Directory for the Year Ending May 1, 1869.* Brooklyn: Lain & Co., 1868.

———. *Brooklyn City Directory for the Year 1884–85.* Brooklyn: Lain & Co., 1884.

———. *Brooklyn City Directory for the Year Ending May 1, 1871.* Brooklyn: Lain & Co., 1870.

———. *Brooklyn City Directory . . . May 1, 1875.* Brooklyn: Lain & Co., 1874.

———. *Brooklyn City Directory . . . May 1, 1876.* Brooklyn: Lain & Co., 1875.

———. *Brooklyn City Directory . . . May 1, 1877.* Brooklyn: Lain & Co., 1876.

———. *Brooklyn City Directory . . . May 1, 1878.* Brooklyn: Lain & Co., 1877.

———. *Brooklyn City Directory . . . May 1, 1879.* Brooklyn: Lain & Co., 1878.

———. *Brooklyn City Directory . . . May 1, 1880.* Brooklyn: Lain & Co., 1879.

———. *Brooklyn City Directory . . . May 1, 1881.* Brooklyn: Lain & Co., 1880.

———. *Brooklyn City Directory . . . May 1, 1882.* Brooklyn: Lain & Co., 1881.

———. *Brooklyn City Directory . . . May 1, 1883.* Brooklyn: Lain & Co., 1882.

Lain, J. *Brooklyn City Directory . . . May 1, 1863.* Brooklyn: J. Lain & Co., 1862.

———. *Brooklyn City Directory . . . May 1, 1867.* Brooklyn: J. Lain & Co., 1866.

"Legal Notices: County Court, Kings County." *The Brooklyn Daily Eagle.* August 16, 1877.

Longworth, Thomas. *Longworth's American Almanac, New-York Register, and City Directory.* New York: Thomas Longworth, 1828.

———. *Longworth's American Almanac . . .* New York: Thomas Longworth, 1829.

———. *Longworth's American Almanac . . .* New York: Thomas Longworth, 1830.

Negro Population 1790–1915. Washington, D.C.: United States Department of Commerce, Bureau of the Census, 1918.

"New York, Marriage Newspaper Extracts, 1801–1880 (Barber Collection)," digital image s.v. "Dr James P Barnett," (publication date January 25, 1878), *Ancestry.com*.

"New York, New York, Extracted Death Index, 1862–1948," s.v. "James Barnett," *Ancestry.com*.

"New York, New York, Index to Death Certificates, 1862–1948," s.v. "Edward Barnett," (died April 7, 1904), *Ancestry.com*.

"New York, Wills and Probate Records, 1659–1999," digital image s.v. "Eliza Barnett" (probate date February 18, 1889), *Ancestry.com*.

"New York Wills and Probate Records, 1659–1999," digital image s.v. "James Barnett" (probate date July 7, 1850), *Ancestry.com*.

"New York, Wills and Probate Records, 1659–1999," digital image s.v. "James P. Barnett," (probate date June 2, 1883), *Ancestry.com*.

New-York Tribune, and James Barnett. "To Let—Two Neat Two-Story, Attic and Basement Houses," *New-York Tribune*, May 10, 1856.

"New York, Wills and Probate Records, 1659–1999," digital image s.v. "Eliza Barnett" (probate date February 18, 1889). *Ancestry.com*.

"Real Estate Transfers [from James P. Barnett]." *Times Union.* November 13, 1879.

"Real Estate Transfers [from Malvina Smith to James P. Barnett]." *The Brooklyn Daily Eagle.* June 2, 1873.

Rutgers Female Institute. *Celebration of the Twenty-Fifth Anniversary of the Rutgers Female Institute.* New York: Rutgers Female Institute, 1864.

———. *Third Annual Circular of the Rutgers Female Institute.* New York, NY: Rutgers Female Institute, 1841.

"Rutgers Female Institute." *The New World* 1, no. 10 (8 August 1840).

Schomburg, Arturo Alfonso. "Dr. James McCune Smith." *Negro History Bulletin* 9, no. 2 (November 1, 1945): 41–42.

Seventeenth Annual Report of the Association for the Benefit of Colored Orphans. New York, NY: Association for the Benefit of Colored Orphans, 1853.

"Supreme Court—Special Term. Before Hon. Judge Roosevelt: A Curious Colored Case." *New York Daily Herald.* April 21, 1853.

University of the City of New-York. *A Catalogue of the Officers and Alumni of the University of the City of New-York.* New York: University of the City of New-York, 1852.

Wilson, Henry, and John F. Trow. *Trow's New York City Directory, Compiled by H. Wilson. For the Year Ending May 1, 1871.* New York: John F. Trow, 1870.

———. *Trow's New York City Directory . . . May 1, 1872.* New York: John F. Trow, 1871.

———. *Trow's New York City Directory . . . May 1, 1873.* New York: John F. Trow, 1872.

———. *Trow's New York City Directory . . . May 1, 1874.* New York: John F. Trow, 1873.

———. *Trow's New York City Directory . . . May 1, 1875.* New York: John F. Trow, 1874.

———. *Trow's New York City Directory . . . May 1, 1876.* New York: John F. Trow, 1875.

———. *Trow's New York City Directory . . . May 1, 1877.* New York: John F. Trow, 1876.

———. *Trow's New-York City Directory . . . May 1, 1867.* New York: John F. Trow, 1866.

———. *Trow's New-York City Directory . . . May 1, 1868.* New York: John F. Trow, 1867.

———. *Trow's New-York City Directory . . . May 1, 1869.* New York: John F. Trow, 1868.

———. *Trow's New-York City Directory . . . May 1, 1870.* New York: John F. Trow, 1869.

———. *Trow's New-York City Directory . . . May 1, 1858.* New York: John F. Trow, 1857.

———. *Trow's New-York City Directory . . . May 1, 1861.* New York: John F. Trow, 1860.

———. *Trow's New-York City Directory . . . May 1, 1862.* New York: John F. Trow, 1861.

———. *Trow's New-York City Directory . . . May 1, 1863.* New York: John F. Trow, 1862.

———. *Trow's New-York City Directory . . . May 1, 1865.* New York: John F. Trow, 1864.

Roots: Tracing the Family History of James McCune and Malvina Barnett Smith, 1783–1937, Part 3

Family of James McCune and Malvina Barnett Smith[1]

The historical record does not reveal the date of James McCune Smith and Malvina Barnett's marriage. There are, however, some clues in the historical record. In an 1859 correspondent's letter for *Frederick Douglass' Paper* (*FDP*), McCune Smith recalled a scene from their early life together; Malvina, as he wrote, was still a teenager when they wed. McCune Smith was about 12 years her senior. Since their first child, Amy, was born in late 1843, they were likely married early that year. In 1840, McCune Smith had moved from 141 Reade to 29 Leonard St, perhaps anticipating their marriage. McCune Smith and Malvina began creating their family at this new home. They were still at 29 Leonard St. when McCune Smith and Malvina invited Gerrit and Elizabeth Smith to join them for tea in late January 1847. Their second child, James Ward, was born there in 1845.[2]

As McCune Smith also recalled in that letter, Malvina decided "two or three years after our 'agreement for better or worse'" that the growing family must move. They joined the crowds who moved in May; most New York City leases expired this month, a tradition carried forward from the city's Dutch origins. McCune Smith recalled house hunting with their first two children in his arms and provisions slung round his neck. Though McCune Smith provided only an approximate year, a New York directory confirms that they had a new address in 1847 at 15 North Moore St. They would remain there until they moved to Williamsburg in the mid-1860s. Malvina gave birth to their next son, Henry M., that year. On May 12, 1848, McCune Smith joyfully reported on the growing family in a letter to friend, mentor, and frequent correspondent Gerrit Smith "I am no longer alone: my wife is a fruitful vine through God's blessing, and three little souls look up to me for support & discipline & guidance: what a holy trust!"[3]

The brick building which housed the Smith family—and an adjoining grocer—welcomed at least seven more children between 1850 and 1852. The first to follow Henry was a daughter, born about February 1850. Sources disagree on her name: an 1850 census and an internment record for the Smith family burial plot at Cypress Hills give her name as Amy G., while a notice in *FDP* gives her name as Anna Gertrude. In March 1852, Peter Williams was followed two years later by Frederick Douglass in April 1854; Mary Maude (variously called Maude Mary) on Sep. 21, 1855; Donald Barnett in the spring of 1858; John Murray in April 1860; and Guy Beaumont in 1862. An 1865 census records that Malvina had ten children in all. However, a handwritten entry in a family bible owned by Smith descendant Antoinette Martignoni states that McCune Smith and Malvina had eleven children. This lost child may have been "Mary S. Smith," a name listed in the internment record above Henry. If she did exist, this suggests that her year of birth was 1846. She appears nowhere else in the historical record, indicating she may not have long survived birth. McCune Smith's mother, Lavinia, and mentor Peter Williams' widow Sarah also joined the household by 1850, as did two boarders.[4] The welcome additions to the Smith family were, however, interspersed with occasions for deep grief.

The discovery that there may have been two Smith daughters named Amy is a poignant reminder of the Smith family's first known great loss. The existence of the eldest is known only from references in three of McCune Smith's letters. The first of these is the only one to reveal her name and dates of birth and death. In 1850, McCune Smith confided his and Malvina's grief to Gerrit Smith, as both friend and fellow father who had suffered the loss of a child, at the "loss of my firstborn, my dear little Amy." She died, McCune Smith wrote, "on Christmas eve, and lacked five days of 6 years of age." Therefore, she was born on Dec. 29, 1843, and died on Dec. 24, 1849. In that letter, McCune Smith marveled at Amy's courage. He would again in "The Black News-Vendor (1852)," his account of a former sailor who had lost his legs following a Christmas Eve shipwreck. In the first of McCune Smith's famed "Heads of the Colored People" series as the New York correspondent for FDP, he wrote:

> *Christmas Eve, two years ago! 1849!"—The tears rushed from my eyes: for on that very night, when the poor sailor struggled with the cold and the storm..., there came into my household a messenger for my first born: sweet, patient little sufferer, after a year of hopes and fears, and deep agony; in the intervals of distress, that day her young hopes were gladdened with tomorrow's Christmas tree and the expected adornings from a mother's loving hand. But long ere midnight came... "the Shadow feared of man.*[5]

Henry's death in 1853 opened a new season of loss for the Smith family; it was announced in FDP on Jun. 10, 1853. He was the subject of two more rare instances of McCune Smith's publicly sharing personal details about his family. He opened his seventh installment of the "Heads" series in early September 1853 with words of mourning for Henry:

> *These sketches were sadly interrupted by the long and painful illness of one whose little grave is filled on the hillside; and again and again... spirit fingers weave his golden hair upon the canvas, and those sad eyes light upon me, and spirit voices break the stillness of the night, in cadences now light and airy, now sobbing in keen agony.*

A letter to editor Horace Greeley of the *New-York Tribune* two years earlier includes an example of McCune Smith's lifelong critique of incoherent popular conceptions of race. In it, McCune Smith brought Henry's fair coloring to bear: Why, he asked, should the "child playing at my elbow ... [who] has a white skin, grey eyes and flaxen hair" be automatically designated black or African when he was of multiracial descent? Such distinctions, arbitrary, and artificial as they were, were used to justify equally arbitrary and irrational forms of injustice and oppression.[6]

1854 took a tremendous toll on the Smith family. On Oct. 6, 1854, in an article for *FDP*, friend and fellow activist Martin Delany listed "beloved and esteemed citizens ... swept away from the shores of time and place by that dread pestilence, the Cholera." Delany included in his list, with their dates of death, "Aug. 13, Frederick Douglass, aged four months and 27 days; Aug. 27, Peter Williams, aged two years and five months; Sep. 19, Anna Gertrude, aged four years, six months and twelve days, children of Melvina and Dr. James McCune Smith." They were victims of the second cholera epidemic that swept New York City in 1832 and 1834. "Anna Gertrude" was the same daughter, based on the given age in Delany's article, like the one the 1850 census and internment record refer to as "Amy G."[7] Delany could have been correct regarding her name, or the census and internment record, or both. If the latter, McCune Smith and Malvina may have memorialized their lost first daughter in the name of another, only later to call her Anna to avoid painful reminders or name confusion. One can only imagine McCune Smith's feelings as a physician as well as a father in losing five children to diseases he could not save them from.

The 1855 New York census, which recorded the Smith household on Jul. 3, shows that the household was then composed mostly of adults, including a servant and four boarders; 9-year-old James Ward was the Smith's only surviving child. It was the only census to assign different races to individual members of the Smith household: it lists

McCune Smith and Lavinia as "mulatto," Malvina with no racial designation, and James Ward as "Light brown." The 1860 and 1865 censuses assign no racial categories to the Smith family. A few months after that 1855 census was taken, daughter Mary Maude Smith was born. On Oct. 6, 1855, McCune Smith wrote excitedly of her arrival to Smith: "We have a renewed blessing in our house in the shape of a little girl who with her mother is doing very well." Malvina had a more challenging time following Donald's birth, as McCune Smith reported to Smith: "I have been very anxious about the health of my wife for the last two months . . . She is better, and in a state of hopeful recovery—with a boy to boot."[8] McCune Smith and Malvina would never again witness the death of their children: James Ward and his four younger siblings born after that terrible summer of 1854 would long survive both their parents.

Throughout the family's years of joy and sorrow, McCune Smith ran a pharmacy and a busy medical practice. He wrote ruefully to Smith that it was often impossible to leave New York City without neglecting his patients' needs; sometimes, these patients included his family, and Smith as well. The medical practice and pharmacy that the newly minted physician established soon after his return to New York City in 1837 on West Broadway, first at number 33, then at 55—occasionally designated 57—after 1847 lasted until the year of his death in 1865. His 19-year-old son James Ward clerked in the pharmacy at least during that last year. McCune Smith ran his practice and pharmacy from the same location initially; when the family moved to 15 N. Moore St., he saw patients in his home office as well. As protégé, friend, and onetime apprentice Philip A. White recalled in 1885, McCune Smith's clients were interracial, "the major portion of his patients being white."[9]

McCune Smith also served as physician to the Colored Orphan Asylum, first officially appointed in 1846. He was associated with the Asylum since about 1838, fundraising, speaking at events, and donating care, the latter at least since 1843.

McCune Smith may have become associated with the Asylum through his mentor Peter Williams, who, as its *Fourth Annual Report* stated, "was among the first to co-operate with the Managers, in laying the foundation of the Asylum." McCune Smith remained the Asylum's chief physician—always at a modest salary—until 1864 when deteriorating health forced him to retire. Throughout those years, McCune Smith continued to fundraise and donate money, treats, and medicine, promoting the Asylum's mission to raise, educate, and train their charges in practical and work skills.[10]

The Smith family also accumulated real estate, which likely contributed to their financial success. Some of their early properties were gifts through Gerrit Smith's land grant scheme—which McCune Smith helped administer—in which the wealthy, white abolitionist donated thousands of acres of land to African Americans New Yorkers, beginning in 1846. The purpose was to help them meet the state's racially discriminatory $250 property requirement while promoting self-sufficiency. However, records show that the Smiths's real estate transactions extended beyond the land grant scheme. An 1860 census reveals that the Smith family were financially secure; it lists their "Value of Real Estate" as $25,000, and their "Value of Personal Estate" as $1500. They retained an Irish servant until at least 1865. By then, their wealth had grown substantially; the *Liberator* reported that McCune Smith was the wealthiest "colored" man in New York City, "being worth about $100,000." The article describes him as having a "good personal appearance," with "a fine and well-developed head, broad and lofty brow, round and full face, firm month, and a bright eye. His complexion is nearly Anglo-Saxon."[11]

McCune Smith was not complacent about his ability to care for his family financially, however. He had long suffered from intermittent ill health—as early as 1841, the editor of *The Colored American* feared for his life. McCune Smith occasionally surmised it might lead to an early death. On Jan. 13, 1864, he wrote to Gerrit Smith.

I have enlarged [sic] heart with an overworked nervous system; and am compelled to be quiet when there is so much to do. It is a hard school but I try and bow. It is a satisfaction, nay a glory, to have lived to see this day, even if I know that I cannot live through it.

Precisely one day less than a year from that letter, McCune Smith, "considering the uncertainty of this present life do therefore make, ordain, publish and declare . . . my last Will and Testament." He appointed Malvina the sole executor of his will and sole guardian of their children. He left her the entire estate except for $100 outright to James Ward, who, at 19, was then their only adult child. She was to manage the estate and support the children until they turned 21. After her death, the remainder was to be divided equally among their surviving children. On Nov. 17, 1865, McCune Smith died at only 52 and was buried in the family plot in Cypress Hills.[12]

As with Lavinia, personal details about Malvina are hard to find. As we have seen, McCune Smith's letters to Gerrit Smith reveal some of Malvina's experiences as wife and mother. His letters also indicate that Malvina expressed her opinions strongly and made decisions for the family, as in the 1847 move. McCune Smith wrote in 1859 that he had only gone to the October 1855 Colored Convention in Philadelphia at Malvina's behest. He did not want to go, he wrote, because he did not think the divided convention could accomplish much. Yet Malvina was insistent: "my better half insisted, as a personal favor that I should go," so, "As a dutiful husband, I went." Malvina also took a "warm interest" in Smith's 1859 offer of a professorship to McCune Smith at New York's Central College, which McCune Smith considered but turned down over financial concerns. McCune Smith's designation of Malvina as sole executor of his will and sole support and guardian of their children further evidence Malvina's leading family role. Other sources provide a few more rare details about Malvina. A report of an 1850 fundraising fair for Frederick Douglass' *The North Star* offered thanks for "the very beautiful screen, worked and presented by Mrs. J. M'Cune Smith." Malvina also contributed to an 1861 fundraiser for the Colored Orphan Asylum. She shared McCune Smith's love of chess; when the first American Chess Conference was held in New York City in October 1857, she insisted they attend. They shared their passion for the game with their children and taught them young. Two of Malvina's personal friends can also be identified. Charlotte Forten Grimké stayed with the Smith family when she visited New York City in 1857. Introduced to the Smiths through Sarah, Peter Williams' widow then living with them, Grimké found a new friend in Malvina. Another is E.E. Howard, who wrote in 1865, "Some books, which I received from a friend in New York, Mrs. Dr. McCune Smith, I desire to acknowledge." In religion, Malvina appears to have been a freethinker, which may explain why she has not been located in church registries after McCune Smith's death. McCune Smith wrote to Gerrit Smith in 1859 that Malvina had become "quite a convert too many of your views;" in *Three Discourses in the Religion of Reason*, Smith espoused forming personal creeds over adhering to institutions or dogma.[13]

Following her husband's death, Malvina continued to live at 162 S. Third St. until at least 1867. From 1870-1879, Malvina lived at 9 Marcy Ave., close to her mother, Eliza. An 1870 census indicates that Malvina's assets were valued at $13,000, far less than what McCune Smith had left her. She was designated "white," as all her children would be in subsequent censuses. By then, the Smith family no longer kept a live-in servant. An 1875 census reveals that the three eldest children still at home had begun working: 19-year-old Mary Maude as a schoolteacher; 17-year-old Donald Barnett as a lawyer's clerk; and 15-year-old John Murray as a printer. Malvina's move from the Third St. house, the loss of their servant, and the children's early forays into the workforce may have resulted from financial difficulties. They might have at least partially resulted from Malvina's continuing, perhaps unwisely, the comfortable upper-middle-class lifestyle she had been accustomed to when McCune Smith, who himself had a taste for luxury, was still alive. In an 1885 interview, Philip A. White, McCune Smith's protégé, friend, and onetime apprentice recalled, "When [McCune Smith] died he left behind him a widow and six children, and $50,000 in money, besides considerable personal property." (There were five surviving children.) He added, disapprovingly, "In a few years, the widow [Malvina] squandered the $50,000 by aping the style of the white aristocracy, and the children are now doing right well." White approved of the latter's hardworking ways, comparing them with their father's: "They are earning their bread by the sweat of their brows."[14]

Malvina may have sought to improve the family finances through real estate transactions in the 1870s, sometimes involving her brother James Parker Barnett. Not all were successful, and not all can be definitively linked to our Malvina since there was more than one Malvina Smith in Brooklyn in the mid-1800s. In 1880, Malvina and her children Mary, John, and Guy—all adults—moved into her mother's house at 117 Penn St. The 1880 census contains a curious entry for the Barnett/Smith household: instead of "Malvina," the census lists a widow "Magreth" as Eliza's daughter, nearly identical in name to Malvina's sister-in-law Margreth. While this may be coincidental—Margreth was not a widow, and she was living with her husband that year—it is notable that that name, so different from "Malvina," was entered. Perhaps Margreth was visiting that day, and the census taker confused her name with Malvina's. Malvina was living at the Penn St. house when she died of uterine cancer on Sep. 13, 1881; she was buried with her husband at Cypress Hills.[15]

Their eldest son, James Ward Smith, attended New York City's male-only Free Academy between 1860–1864, receiving a thorough liberal arts education, including classics studies, which his father also had specialized in. Though he excelled there, he did not re-enroll in autumn 1864. James clerked at his father's pharmacy in 1865; he may have decided that his time was better spent there during McCune Smith's last illness. He may also appear in an undated letter: a cousin of Rebecca Downing, daughter of McCune Smith's friend George T. Downing, wrote, "Your very particular friend Jim Smith was there, looking as mischievous as ever. I . . . said nothing to betray you or Delie." If this indeed refers to James, he ultimately found romance elsewhere. The historical record does not tell us what took him to Woodbridge, New Jersey, but it does reveal that he married Chloe Luchera Day there on Jun. 23, 1868. James also found work there as a schoolteacher. By 1874, he, Chloe, and their two sons had moved to Newark, where the family would remain. From 1875–1886, James would serve as principal for two Newark primary schools; Chloe would join him in that profession in 1880. In 1886, James started a business as a general broker at 802 Broad St. while serving as principal of an evening school. The timing coincided with his uncle James Parker's death in February 1886; James was left $1,000 in his will. By the next year, James was no longer working as an educator; his business now employed him full-time. His son Walter would join the firm as a partner in 1900. He died on Feb. 10, 1917. When Chloe died in 1922, she was buried with him at Oakwood Cemetery in South Granville, New York, home to Chloe's family since the Revolutionary War era.[16]

McCune Smith and Malvina's next surviving child, Mary Maude Smith, has proven the most elusive to research. She is designated by various combinations of "Mary," "Maude," "Maud," and "M" Smith in family and other verifiable records, which may help explain the difficulty locating her elsewhere. (This article, for space considerations, will only discuss sources most likely to refer to her). The historical record may reveal most about Mary Maude's educational and professional career. A "Maude M. Smith" of Brooklyn was enrolled at the female-only Packer Collegiate Institute in 1873–1874. An 1875 census lists 19-year-old "Maud Smith" as a schoolteacher. She may have continued her training at the Normal College of the City of New York in 1876. Inspired by the James Ward's alma mater, the Free Academy, the all-female Normal College was founded to provide tuition-free high school and college-level courses and intensive training for educators. Mary Maude reemerges in the historical record in an 1880 census as a schoolteacher, then unemployed. By 1889, she may have been a member of the Queens County Teachers' Institute. She appears in uncle James Parker's 1883 will and an 1889 probate document for grandmother Eliza's will, living with brothers Donald and Guy at 128 State St. in Brooklyn. Mary Maude is also recorded in a 1900 census entry—which contains many errors—for Donald's household, now on Lefferts Ave, and again in a schoolteacher retirement list for 1915. Mary Maude is listed in telephone directories between 1917–1928, still at Lefferts Ave. The historical record had not yielded any further insights into Mary Maude's life before she died on June 9, 1931, at her nephew Henry W. Smith's house at 353 Autumn Ave. She was buried in the Cypress Hills family plot.[17]

The historical record reveals much about the life of Donald Barnett Smith. He also began working early: an 1875 census lists 17-year-old Donald as a clerk in a Brooklyn lawyer's office. He also married early: at 19, he wed Marie Munn Baker in Manhattan on Nov. 4, 1877. The newlyweds did not establish their independence immediately: Donald is listed in an 1879 Brooklyn directory at his mother's address. They may have decided to wait until Donald completed his training; he was admitted to the bar in September 1879. An 1880 census lists Donald and Marie as boarders in another's home. Donald and Marie's marriage did not last long: they divorced in 1881. From 1886 to at least 1889, Donald lived with sister Mary Maude and brother Guy after which he briefly lived in Newark, probably in James Ward's household. By 1896, Donald established his law practice at Brooklyn's Court Square; directories for 1898 and 1899 list him at Morris Park, Long Island. Donald married his second wife, a widow and mother of a 9-year-old son Anna Marie Crotty (née Adams) in 1899. Donald and Anna remained in Brooklyn for the rest of their lives. Donald's legal career was, overall, very successful. His practice focused on civil, property, and family law.[18]

Athletics were among Donald Barnett's abiding interests. He was a member of the Williamsburg Athletic Club in the early 1880s, as were his younger brothers John and Guy. They would regularly attend its annual reunion events for the rest of their lives. In 1913, Anna died of heart disease and was buried at Holy Cross, a Roman Catholic cemetery. When Donald Barnett died on Oct. 27, 1927, he was buried five miles away in the family plot at Cypress Hills, indicating he did not convert to Anna's faith. They had no known children together.[19]

McCune Smith and Malvina's next surviving child, John Murray Smith, was named for John Murray, McCune Smith's fellow abolitionist and friend. Like Mary Maude and Donald, John began working early, at 15, as a printer, a profession he kept until at least mid-1880. John next appears in the historical record in the 1885 Florida census, in Orange County; the 1889 probate document for Eliza's will specifies he lived in Eustis. While his new profession as an orange grower met with mixed success, John met two people who would profoundly affect his life. The first of these was Henry Wickham Hore, a 52-year-old bachelor and naturalized citizen of English origin who lived with John. Records do not tell us whether the elder Hore was an employer, mentor, co-worker, or friend to John, but they remained closely connected, as we shall see. The second was Annie Lenore Shroy, a white Philadelphia-born servant in the neighboring Rohrer family household. John and Annie married no later than mid-1888; their three children were born in Eustis. About 1897, the family relocated to Brooklyn, accompanied by Hore, and settled at 153 Garfield Place. John resumed work as a printer, the occupation that he would keep for the rest of his working life. By December of that year, John was a fraternal society member and served as a deacon for St. Matthew's Lutheran Church.[20]

1914 was likely the most painful year of John Murray's life. On Mar. 28, Hore died. A few days before his death, Hore made a will leaving his Florida real estate "to my friend John Murray Smith . . . for the care and attention he has given me and the kindness he has shown me during the thirty years I have lived with him as a member of his family." Hore made John sole executor of his will. His funeral services were held at the family church, St. Matthews, and he was buried in the Barnett-Smith family plot at Cypress Hills. Given the ways Hore, John, and John's family shared their lives, home, and fortunes, it is likely that Hore, who never fathered children himself, played a fatherly role to the man who had lost own his father so early and a grandfatherly role to his children. Just under one year later, on Mar. 30, 1915, John's wife Annie died of "heart trouble." Her funeral services were also held at St. Matthew's, and she was buried in the family plot in Cypress Hills. Besides his attendance at Williamsburgh Athletic Club reunion events, John disappears from the historical record until newspapers announced his death on May 12, 1922; he was buried with his wife.[21]

Guy Beaumont Smith, born three years before McCune Smith's death, was the least likely of the children to have memories of his father. However, he carried on McCune Smith's legacy in at least one respect: an 1880 census lists eighteen-year-old Guy as a "drug clerk." He would continue in this industry until at least 1894. Directories list Guy as a salesman or agent in an unspecified industry from 1896–1908; a 1905 census identifies one as "Insulation." Throughout most of the 1880s, Guy, still single, lived with the family in Brooklyn. In 1889 or shortly after that, Guy married a widow and mother of a 9-year-old son, Elizabeth Agnes Donegan (née Riley). A handwritten entry in the family bible owned by Guy's granddaughter Antoinette Martignoni provides the date of their marriage: Aug. 7, 1889. Guy and Elizabeth had four children together who survived infancy.[22] The family became prominent members in Brooklyn society: they regularly attended balls, fundraisers, lectures, and theater, at times appearing in stage productions themselves.[23] By 1910, Guy turned his job in the insulation industry into a career as a refrigeration engineer. After his retirement about 1925, he and Elizabeth lived at least part of the year at the family's mountain retreat in Hunter, in the Catskills, upstate New York. Guy appears to have converted to Elizabeth's Catholic religion following their marriage. When Guy died in Brooklyn on Mar. 13, 1935, a requiem mass was held for him at Holy Innocents Roman Catholic Church; like his sister-in-law Anna, he was buried at Holy Cross Cemetery.[24] Elizabeth died seven months later, on Oct. 25, 1937, at the family's Hunter home. Her funeral mass was also held at Holy Innocents, and she was also buried at Holy Cross.[25]

Conclusion

The Smith and Barnett family histories reveal difficulties and complexities inherent in living in a racially discriminatory and stratified society and the various ways in which the families and their members navigated them. Over time, the Smith and Barnett families were identified variously in public records, trending from "mulatto" to "white." Scholar John Stauffer argues that one reason James McCune Smith's legacy has been widely forgotten is that

> McCune Smith's descendants wanted him erased from the historical record. McCune Smith was light-skinned and could have passed for white. His wife, Malvina Barnet, was also light-skinned, as were their children, and within a few years of his death, they did pass for white. Passing required them to bury the facts of his existence.[26]

However, the historical record does not necessarily support this harsh assessment of the families' intentions regarding McCune Smith's memory. For example, as this article demonstrates in Part I, racial identification in censuses depended on the census taker's perception, not self-identification. The 1860 federal and 1865 state censuses for McCune Smith and Malvina's family indicate that the census takers perceived no nonwhite ancestry by the omission of racial categorization. Even McCune Smith, proud as he was of his African ancestry, apparently did not insist on their being identified accordingly, and almost certainly was not asked. The latter is likely true for all other census entries for the Barnett and Smith family members.

The historical record also indicates that Malvina and, later, their children witnessed McCune Smith's struggle for racial justice firsthand. They observed him triumphant at times and doggedly persistent at others. They also saw his periods of depression when the struggle for racial justice sometimes appeared futile, and how McCune Smith endured these obstacles as he suffered from the ill health that increasingly left him confined, unwillingly, to the house. Given the mental and physical sufferings of husband and father, Malvina and her children may have wanted to spare themselves and their children the suffering and lack of opportunity that would have accompanied insistence on claiming African heritage. From his childhood onward, McCune Smith was forced to struggle against racial discrimination and injustice. But for his descendants and other extended family members, peace and opportunity were relatively easy to attain: to all outward appearances, they were white.

Yet there is no evidence to suggest that McCune Smith's children actively rejected their father's legacy or attempted to distance themselves from his memory: he is identified as Guy Beaumont's father in his obituary, named as an ancestor in the family bible, and many among his descendants and extended family were buried near him in the family plot in Cypress Hills. However, his wife and children did not actively promote his legacy, as the family of his friend and colleague Frederick Douglass did for him after his death.

The Smith and Barnett family stories, instead, represent the starkness of a choice that so many whose African ancestry was not evident to others would have faced: identify this ancestry in a racially stratified society, often at a high cost to self and family, or let that identity go so they and their children could enjoy lives of opportunity, peace, and safety.

As Allyson V. Hobbs writes in *A Chosen Exile: A History of Racial Passing in American Life*, "To pass as white was to make an anxious decision to turn one's back on a black racial identity and to claim to belong to a group to which one was not legally assigned." While members of the Smith and Barnett families may have decided to "pass" as Hobbs describes, this article has found no direct evidence of this. However, the evidence does reveal that the Smith and Barnett families often faced "predicaments of those who could pass as white" and, at the very least, simply allowed others to make assumptions about their identity, as Malvina and James Parker had in their youth.[27] Following McCune Smith's death, McCune Smith's widow's and children's desire for the safety and security that accompanied a white identity may indeed help explain why McCune Smith's passionate and turbulent life of resistance, struggle, and transcendence came to be so widely forgotten, unintentional as that result may have been. In any case, this article seeks to contribute to restoring the lost history of the Smith and Barnett families, to their descendants, to scholarship, and public memory.

ENDNOTES

1. See "Tracing the Family History" Part One for the family tree accompanying this article series.

2. James McCune Smith, letter to the editor, *FDP*, Apr. 29, 1859; James McCune Smith to Gerrit Smith, Feb. 6, 1850, GSP; Thomas Longworth, *Longworth's American Almanac, New-York Register, and City Directory* (NY: Thomas Longworth, 1839), 603; Longworth, *Longworth's*, 1840, 581; 1850 United States Census, NY, NY County, NY, digital image s.v. "James McCune Smith," *FamilySearch.org*; 1855 NY State Census, NY, NY County, digital image s.v. "James McCune Smith." "James Ward Smith (1845–1917)," Find a Grave, accessed Jan. 10, 2019, https://www.findagrave.com/memorial/35915727/james-ward-smith; James McCune Smith to Gerrit Smith, Jan. 25, 1847, GSP; Octavius B. Frothingham, *Gerrit Smith: A Biography* (NY: G.P. Putnam's Sons, 1878), 19.

3. Edwin G. Burrows and Mike Wallace. *Gotham: A History of New York City To 1898* (NY: Oxford University Press, 1998), 392; John Doggett, *Doggett's New-York City Directory, for 1847 & 1848* (NY: John Doggett, Jr., 1847), 378; James McCune Smith to Gerrit Smith, May 12, 1848, GSP.

4. Delany, Martin R. "Died." *FDP*, Oct. 6, 1854.; 'Frederick Douglass Smith (1854–1854)'; 1860 US Census, NY, NY County, NY, digital image s.v. "Jas. M. Smith." *Family Search.org*; "Maude Mary Smith (1856–1931)," Find a Grave, accessed Jan. 10, 2019. https://www.findagrave.com/memorial/167432432/maude-mary-smith; "Donald B Smith (1858–1927)," Find a Grave, accessed Apr. 24, 2020. https://www.findagrave.com/memorial/167433190/donald-b-smith; 1865 NY State Census, NY, NY County, digital image s.v. "James M. Smith," *FamilySearch.org*.; "Guy B Smith (1861–1935)," Find a Grave, accessed Jan. 10, 2019. https://www.findagrave.com/memorial/114085944/guy-b-smith; Family Bible of Antoinette Martignoni, Great-Granddaughter of James McCune Smith, n.d.; "Interment Record for Smith Family Plot at Cypress Hills Cemetery," n.d.

5. James McCune Smith to Gerrit Smith, Feb. 6, 1850, GSP; McCune Smith, *Works*, 193.

6. "We Learn with Sincere Regret...," *FDP*, Jun. 10, 1853; McCune Smith, Works, 217; James McCune Smith, "African Colonisation—The Other Side." *National Anti-Slavery Standard*, Aug. 28, 1851.

7. Delany, "Died;" Burrows and Wallace, *Gotham*, 589, 595; "Internment Record."

8. James McCune Smith to Gerrit Smith, Oct. 6, 1855; Apr. 9, 1858, GSP.

9. James McCune Smith to Gerrit Smith, Dec. 17/18 1846; Dec. 28/30/31 1846; Mar. 22, 1848; May 12, 1848; Mar. 1/31, 1855; and Sep. 20, 1859, GSP; "Medical Consultations," The Colored American, Nov. 11, 1837; "Drugs and Medicines." *The Colored American*, Nov. 11, 1837; Longworth, *Longworth's*, 1843, 313; Doggett, NY City Directory, 322; Henry Wilson, *Wilson's Business Directory of NYC* (NY: John F. Trow, 1856), 128, 319; "Colored Men as Physicians," *Nemaha County Republican*, Mar. 19, 1885.

10. "The Managers of the Colored Orphan Asylum..." NY Journal of Commerce, Mar. 23, 1841; "The Sixth Anniversary of the Colored Orphan Asylum," *The Evening Post*, Dec. 12, 1842; Seventh Annual Report of the ABCO (NY: ABCO, 1843), 6; Tenth Annual Report of the ABCO, 1846, 2; Twenty-Third Annual Report of the ABCO, 1860, 3, 12, 16, 22, 24; Twenty-Fourth Annual Report of the ABCO, 1861, 3, 5–6, 11–12, 17–18, 25; Twenty-Fifth Annual Report of the ABCO, 1862, 3, 11–12, 19–20; Twenty-Sixth Annual Report of the ABCO, 1863, 3, 5–6, 12–14, 21; Twenty-Seventh Annual Report of the ABCO, 1864, 3, 14, 17, 27; Twenty-Ninth Annual Report of the ABCO, 1865, 6.

11. James McCune Smith, Theodore S. Wright, and Charles B. Ray, *An Address to the Three Thousand Colored Citizens of New-York...*, Gerrit Smith, 1846, 3–7, 9; James McCune Smith to Gerrit Smith, Dec. 17/18, 1846; Dec. 28/30/31, 1846; Mar. 22, 1848; May 12, 1848; and Jul. 7, 1848, GSP; Sally E. Svenson, *Blacks in the Adirondacks* (Syracuse: Syracuse University Press, 2017), 19–20; "NY Land Records, 1630–1975," "Smith, James McCune;" "NY Land Records, 1630–1975," "Smith, James M.C./Malvina, His Wife:" Guido Furman, "Obituary of James McCune Smith," *The Medical Register of the City of New York for the Year Commencing Jun. 1, 1866*, 1866, 202; "The Negroes of New York," *The Liberator*, Aug. 25, 1865.

12. "Afflicting," *The Colored American*, Dec. 4, 1841; James McCune Smith to Gerrit Smith, May 12, 1848, GSP; *Twenty-Seventh Annual Report*, 17; James McCune Smith to Gerrit Smith, with a note by Frederick Douglass, Jan. 13, 1864, GSP; James McCune Smith to Gerrit Smith, Apr. 26, 1864, GSP; *Twenty-Eighth Annual Report*, 5–7; James McCune Smith to Gerrit Smith, Feb. 17, 1865, GSP; "NY Probate Records, 1629–1971 - KC - Wills," digital image s.v. "James McCune Smith;" Furman, "Obituary;" "Dr. James McCune Smith (1813–1865)," Find a Grave, accessed Jan. 10, 2019. https://www.findagrave.com/memorial/59240574/james-mccune-smith.

13. James McCune Smith, letter to the editor, *FDP*, Jan. 21, 1859; James McCune Smith to Gerrit Smith, Jan. 29, 1859; Mar. 9, 1859, GSP; Fanny Tompkins, "Report of the North Star Fair in New York," *The North Star*, Jun. 20, 1850; *Twenty-Fifth Annual Report*, 21; McCune Smith, *Works*, 284-85; Charlotte Forten Grimké. *The Journals of Charlotte Forten Grimké*. Edited by Brenda E. Stevenson (NY/Oxford: Oxford University Press, 1988), 241, 579 n45; E. E. Howard, E. E. "Progress Among the Freedmen." *The Christian Recorder*. Nov. 25, 1865; James McCune Smith to Gerrit Smith, Sep. 20, 1859, 1850; Gerrit Smith, *Three Discourses on the Religion of Reason* (NY: Ross & Tousey, 1859), 4, 23, 45–47.

14 George T. Lain, *Brooklyn City Directory for the Year Ending May 1, 1868* (Brooklyn: J. Lain & Co., 1867), 574; Lain, *Brooklyn City Directory*, 1870, 671; 1875 NY State Census, Brooklyn, KC, digital image s.v. "Eliza Barnett," Ancestry.com; 1870 US Census, Brooklyn, KC, NY, digital image s.v. "Malvina Smith," Ancestry.com; KY, digital image s.v. "Malvina Smith," Ancestry.com; William J. Wilson, letter to the editor, *FDP*, Jan. 26, 1855; George T. Downing, letter to the editor, *FDP*, Mar. 7, 1856; "Colored Men as Physicians."

15 "Real Estate Transfers," *TBDE*, Jun. 2, 1873; "Legal Notices: County Court, KC," *TBDE*, Aug. 16, 1877: Lain, *Brooklyn City Directory*, 1880, 40, 1020; 1880 US Census, Brooklyn, KC, NY, digital image s.v. "Eliza Barnet," Ancestry.com; "NY, NY, Index to Death Certificates, 1862–1948," s.v. "Melvina Smith." Ancestry.com.

16 *Twelfth Annual Report on the Operations and Condition of the Free Academy . . . , July 1860* (NY: FACNY, 1860), 67; *Twelfth Annual Register of the FACNY, 1860–1861* (NY: FACNY, 1862), 99; *Thirteenth Annual Register of the FACNY, 1861–1862* (NY: FACNY, 1861), 99; *Merit Roll of the FACNY, First Academic Term* (NY: FACNY, 1862), 15; *Fourteenth Annual Register of the FACNY, 1862–1863* (NY: FACNY, 1862), 93; *Fifteenth Annual Register of the FACNY, 1863–1864* (NY: FACNY, 1863), 93; "Letter from Cousin Louise to Rebecca M. Downing," undated, George T. Downing Papers. Moorland-Spingarn Research Center, Howard University ("Delie" probably refers to Rebecca's sister Cordelia); "NJ, Marriage Records, 1670–1965," s.v. "Chloe Luchera Day." Ancestry.com; 1870 US Census, Woodbridge, Middlesex County, NJ, digital image s.v. "James W. Smith," Ancestry.com; Holbrook, A. Stephen. *Holbrook's Newark City and Business Directory Official for the Year Ending Apr. 1, 1875* (Newark: A. Stephen Holbrook, 1874), 679; Holbrook, *Holbrook's*, 1875, 696, 888; Holbrook, *Holbrook's*, 1880, 745, 944; "NY Wills, 1659–1999," "James P. Barnett;" *Holbrook's*, 1901, 1025, 1026; 1880 US Census, "James W. Smith;" 1885 NJ State Census, Newark, Essex County, digital image s.v. "James W. Smith," Ancestry.com; 1900 US Census, Newark, Essex County, NJ, digital image s.v. "James W Smith," Ancestry.com; 1910 US Census, Newark, Essex County, NJ, digital image s.v. "James W. Smith," Ancestry.com; 1915 NJ State Census, Newark, Essex County, digital image s.v. "J. Ward Smith," Ancestry.com; "North America, Family Histories, 1500–2000," digital image s.v. "Mrs. Chloe L. Day Smith" (Lineage Book, National Society of the Daughters of the American Revolution). Ancestry.com; "James Ward Smith (1845–1917);" "Chloe L. Day Smith (1847–1922)," Find a Grave, accessed Jan. 10, 2019, https://www.findagrave.com/memorial/35915740/chloe-l_-smith.

17 *Circular and Catalogue of the Packer Collegiate Institute* (NY: Packer Collegiate Institute, 1874), 30; *Annual Report of the President of the Normal College [of the City of New York] for the Year Ending Dec. 31, 1876* (NY: NYC Normal College, 1877), 13, 20, 71; "NY Wills, 1659–1999," "James P. Barnett;" "NY, Wills and Probate Records, 1659–1999," digital image s.v. "Eliza Barnett" (petition of Edmund W. Barnett), Ancestry.com; "Queens County Teachers' Institute," *TBDE*, Apr. 25, 1889; 1900 US Census, NY, Queens County, NY, digital image s.v. "Donald Smith." Ancestry.com; "NYC, Public School Teacher Retirement List, 1895–1915," s.v. "Maud M. Smith." Ancestry.com; *NYC Telephone Directory*, Oct. 11, 1917, 911; *NYC Telephone Directory*, May 15, 1920, 1147; *NYC Telephone Directory*, 1924, 666; *NYC Telephone Directory*, Oct. 7, 1925, 770; *NYC Telephone Directory*, 1926, 835; *NYC Telephone Directory*, Summer 1927, 917; *NYC Telephone Directory*, 1928, 1017; "NY, NY, Index to Death Certificates, 1862–1948: Brooklyn: 1931," s.v. "Maude Mary Smith," Ancestry.com."

18 "NY, NYC Marriage Records, 1829–1940," s.v. "Marie Munn Baker." FamilySearch.org; "Personal: Smith," *Times Union*, Sep. 13, 1879; 1880 US Census, "Donald Smith;" "Divorce Granted." *The Brooklyn Union*, Nov. 7, 1881; Lain and Healy, *Brooklyn City Directory*, 1896, 1378; Lain and Healy, *Brooklyn City Directory*, 1899, 1314; 1910 US Census, NY, Brooklyn, KC, NY, digital image s.v. "Donald Smith." Ancestry.com; 1920 US Census, NY, Brooklyn, KC, NY, digital image s.v. "Donald Smith," Ancestry.com; "The People of the State of New York," *TBDE*, Nov. 20, 1900; Upington, *Upington's Brooklyn Directory*, 1901, 1210; Upington, Upington, *Upington's*, 1908, 926; "County Court, County of Kings," *TBDE*, Apr. 26, 1907; "Verdict for $2,550," *The Brooklyn Citizen*, Feb. 19, 1909; "Client Accuses Lawyer," *Times Union*, Sep. 4, 1909; "Held for Wrong Registry," *TBDE*, Nov. 5, 1918; "Court Frees Five Men Accused of Auto Theft," *TSU*, Dec. 11, 1918; "Notice of Sale," *TSU*, Dec. 17, 1919; "Legal Notices," *The Brooklyn Citizen*, Feb. 23, 1926; *NYC Telephone Directory*, Oct. 14,

1915, 774; *NYC Telephone Directory*, Oct. 7, 1925, 767; *NYC Telephone Directory*, 1926, 832; *NYC Telephone Directory*, Summer 1927, 914.

19. "WAC Reunion." *Times Union*, Jan. 23, 1899; "Memories Are Revived of Williamsburg AC" *TBDE*, Feb. 17, 1908; "Veteran Athletes Hold Big Reunion Dinner," *TBDE*, Mar. 18, 1912; "Old-Time Athletes' Reunion." *The Chat*, Feb. 26, 1916; "Old Timers' Reunion Dinner," *The Chat*, Apr. 6, 1918; "Athletes Once Famous Dine," *Times Union*, Mar. 2, 1919; "Alumni Association Holds Twenty-Eighth Reunion," *TSU*, Mar. 11, 1925; "Old Williamsburg AC Holds Reunion Dinner," *The Brooklyn Citizen*, Mar. 8, 1926; Frederick William Janssen, *History of American Amateur Athletics* (NY: C.R. Bourne, 1885), 13, 15, 26; "Anna M.C. Smith," *TSU*, Oct. 29, 1913; "Mrs. A. M. Smith Dies." *The Brooklyn Citizen*, Oct. 29, 1913; "Donald B Smith (1858-1927)."

20. James McCune Smith, "John Murray (of Glasgow)," in *Autographs for Freedom*, 1:62–67 (Boston: John P. Jewett and Co., 1853); "1880 US Census, "Eliza Barnet;" 1885 FL State Census, Orange County, digital image s.v. "J. M. Smith," *Ancestry.com*; "'NY Wills, 1659–1999," "Eliza Barnett" (petition); 1900 US Census, NY, Brooklyn, KC, NY, digital image s.v. "John M. Smith." *Ancestry.com*; Lain and Healy, *Lain & Healy's*, 1899, 1320; 1905 NY State Census, NY, Brooklyn, KC, digital image s.v. "Murry J Smith," *Ancestry.com*; 1910 US Census, NY, Brooklyn, KC, NY, digital image s.v. "John M. Smith," *Ancestry.com*;

21. "Henry Wickham Hore," *TBDE*, Mar. 30, 1914; "Florida, Wills and Probate Records, 1810–1974," digital image s.v. "Henry Wickham Hore," *Ancestry.com*; Interment Record;" "Obituary: Mrs. Annie Lenore Smith;" "Smith - John Murray Smith," *TBDE*, May 11, 1922.

22. 1865 NY State Census, "James M. Smith" (Guy is designated "George" in this census, the first public record he appears in. He may have been named this originally, or the census taker may have erred) 1880 US Census, "Eliza Barnet" (Guy is designated "Duibe" in this census. Whether this was also an error or the census taker was annoyed, the historical record does not reveal); Lain and Healy, *Brooklyn City Directory*, 1896, 1981; 1900 US Census, NY, Queens County, NY, digital image s.v. "Guy Smith," *Ancestry.com*.; Upington, *Upington's Brooklyn Directory*, 1901, 1212; 1905 NY State Census, NY, Brooklyn, KC, digital image s.v. "Guy Smith," *Ancestry.com*.; Upington, *Upington's*, 1908, 928; Lain, *Brooklyn City Directory*, 1888, 1119; "NY Wills, 1659–1999," "Eliza Barnett" (petition); "Episcopal Diocese of NY Church Records, 1767–1970," "Guy Beaumont Smith;" *Family Bible*; 1910 US Census, NY, Brooklyn, KC, NY, digital image s.v. "Guy B Smith," *Ancestry.com*; 1915 NY State Census, NY, Brooklyn, KC, digital image s.v. "Guy Smith," *Ancestry.com*; 1920 US Census, NY, Brooklyn, KC, digital image s.v. "Guy B Smith," *Ancestry.com*; 1925 NY State Census, Hunter, Greene County, digital image s.v. "Guy B Smith," *Ancestry.com*; 1930 US Census, Hunter, Greene County, NY, digital image s.v. "Guy B Smith," *Ancestry.com*; "Rites Tomorrow for Mrs. E. A. Smith," *TBDE*, Oct. 28, 1937.

23. "Park Theater," *TBDE*, Dec. 2, 1892;" "Easter Bazaar and Sale," *The Brooklyn Citizen*, Mar. 23, 1907;" "Brooklyn Society: Who's Who at St. Mary's...," *TBDE*, May 3, 1908;" "Brooklyn Society [The Cathedral Club]," *TBDE*, May 24, 1909;" "Doings in Society and Catholic Clubdom," *The Tablet*, Dec. 2, 1911;" "The Visitation's Very Excellent Theatre Party," *Times Union*, Oct. 25, 1927."

24. "Guy B. Smith."

25. "Smith - Elizabeth A," *TBDE*, Oct. 28, 1937; "Elizabeth A. Smith (1858–1937)," Find a Grave, accessed Jan. 10, 2019. https://www.findagrave.com/memorial/84756532/elizabeth-a_-smith.

26. McCune Smith, *Works*, xvi.

27. Allyson Vanessa Hobbs, *A Chosen Exile: A History of Racial Passing in American Life* (Cambridge: Harvard University Press, 2014), 5.

BIBLIOGRAPHY

To condense citations generated by the in-depth genealogical research presented, this article employs the abbreviations below and standard abbreviations for place names and dates.

ABCO: Association for the Benefit of Colored Orphans
FACNY: Free Academy of the City of New York
FDP: *Frederick Douglass's Paper*
KC: Kings County
TBDE: *The Brooklyn Daily Eagle*
TSU: *The Standard Union*
Manuscript Collection: Gerrit Smith Papers. Syracuse University Libraries (GSP).

1850 US Census, NY, NY County, NY, digital image s.v. "James McCune Smith." *FamilySearch.org*.

1855 NY State Census, NY, NY County, digital image s.v. "James McCune Smith." *FamilySearch.org*.

1860 US Census, NY, NY County, NY, digital image s.v. "Jas. M. Smith." *FamilySearch.org*.

1865 NY State Census, NY, NY County, digital image s.v. "James M. Smith." *FamilySearch.org*.

1870 US Census, Brooklyn, KC, NY, digital image s.v. "Malvina Smith." *Ancestry.com*.

1870 US Census, Woodbridge, Middlesex County, NJ, digital image s.v. "James W. Smith." *Ancestry.com*.

1875 NY State Census, Brooklyn, KC, digital image s.v. "Eliza Barnett." *Ancestry.com*.

1875 NY State Census, Brooklyn, KC, digital image s.v. "Malvina Smith." *Ancestry.com*.

1880 US Census, Brooklyn, KC, NY, digital image s.v. "Donald Smith." *Ancestry.com*.

1880 US Census, Brooklyn, KC, NY, digital image s.v. "Eliza Barnet." *Ancestry.com*.

1880 US Census, Newark, Essex County, NJ, digital image s.v. "James W. Smith." *Ancestry.com*.

1885 FL State Census, Orange County, digital image s.v. "J. M. Smith." *Ancestry.com*.

1885 NJ State Census, Newark, Essex County, digital image s.v. "James W. Smith." *Ancestry.com*.

1900 US Census, NY, Brooklyn, KC, NY, digital image s.v. "John M. Smith." *Ancestry.com*.

1900 US Census, NY, Queens County, NY, digital image s.v. "Donald Smith." *Ancestry.com*.

1900 US Census, NY, Queens County, NY, digital image s.v. "Guy Smith." *Ancestry.com*.

1900 US Census, Newark, Essex County, NJ, digital image s.v. "James W Smith." *Ancestry.com*.

1905 NY State Census, NY, Brooklyn, KC, NY, digital image s.v. "Guy Smith." *Ancestry.com*.

1905 NY State Census, NY, Brooklyn, KC, NY, digital image s.v. "Murry J Smith." *Ancestry.com*.

1910 US Census, NY, Brooklyn, KC, NY, digital image s.v. "Donald Smith." *Ancestry.com*.

1910 US Census, NY, Brooklyn, KC, NY, digital image s.v. "Guy B Smith." *Ancestry.com*.

1910 US Census, NY, Brooklyn, KC, NY, digital image s.v. "John M. Smith." *Ancestry.com*.

1910 US Census, Newark, Essex County, NJ, digital image s.v. "James W Smith." *Ancestry.com*.

1915 NJ State Census, Newark, Essex County, digital image s.v. "J. Ward Smith." *Ancestry.com*.

1915 NY State Census, NY, Brooklyn, KC, NY, digital image s.v. "Guy Smith." *Ancestry.com*.

1920 US Census, NY, Brooklyn, KC, NY, digital image s.v. "Guy B Smith." *Ancestry.com*.

1920 US Census, NY, Brooklyn, KC, NY, digital image s.v. "Donald Smith." *Ancestry.com*.

1925 NY State Census, Hunter, Greene County, digital image s.v. "Guy B Smith." *Ancestry.com*.

1930 US Census, Hunter, Greene County, NY, digital image s.v. "Guy B Smith." *Ancestry.com*.

"Afflicting." *The Colored American*. Dec. 4, 1841.

"Alumni Association Holds Twenty-Eighth Reunion" *TSU*. Mar. 11, 1925.

"Anna M.C. Smith." *TSU*. Oct. 29, 1913.

Annual Report of the President of the Normal College [of the City of New York] for the Year Ending Dec. 31, 1876. New York: New York City Normal College, 1877.

"Athletes Once Famous Dine." *Times Union*. Mar. 2, 1919.

Blight, David. W. "In Search of Learning, Liberty, and Self Definition: James McCune Smith and the Ordeal of the Antebellum Black Intellectual." *Afro-Americans in New York Life and History* 9, no. 2 (1985): 7–26.

"Brooklyn Society [The Cathedral Club]." *TBDE*. May 24, 1909.

"Brooklyn Society: Who's Who at St. Mary's . . ." *TBDE*. May 3, 1908.

Burrows, Edwin G., and Mike Wallace. *Gotham: A History of New York City To 1898*. New York: Oxford University Press, 1998.

Find a Grave. "Chloe L. Day Smith (1847–1922)." Accessed Jan. 10, 2019. https://www.findagrave.com/memorial/35915740/chloe-l_-smith.

Circular and Catalogue of the Packer Collegiate Institute. New York: Packer Collegiate Institute, 1874.

"Client Accuses Lawyer: Donald B. Smith . . . " *Times Union*. Sep. 4, 1909.

"Colored Men as Physicians." *Nemaha County Republican*. Mar. 19, 1885.

"County Court, County of Kings." *TBDE*. Apr. 26, 1907.

"Court Frees Five Men Accused of Auto Theft." *TSU*. Dec. 11, 1918.

Delany, Martin R. "Died." *FDP*. Oct. 6, 1854.

"Divorce Granted." *The Brooklyn Union*. Nov. 7, 1881.

Doggett, John. *Doggett's New-York City Directory, for 1847 & 1848*. NY: John Doggett, 1847.

———. *The New-York City Directory, for 1844 & 1845*. New York: John Doggett, 1844.

"Doings in Society and Catholic Clubdom." *The Tablet*. Dec. 2, 1911.

Find a Grave. "Donald B Smith (1858-1927)." Accessed Apr. 24, 2020. https://www.findagrave.com/memorial/167433190/donald-b-smith.

"Donald B. Smith Beats Gus Oberland..." *TBDE*. Dec. 4, 1911.

Downing, George T. Letter to the editor. *FDP*. Mar. 7, 1856.

Find a Grave. "Dr. James McCune Smith (1813–1865)." Accessed Jan. 10, 2019. https://www.findagrave.com/memorial/59240574/james-mccune-smith.

"Drugs and Medicines." *The Colored American*. Nov. 11, 1837.

"Easter Bazaar and Sale." *The Brooklyn Citizen*. Mar. 23, 1907.

Find a Grave. "Elizabeth A. Smith (1858–1937)." Accessed Jan. 10, 2019. https://www.findagrave.com/memorial/84756532/elizabeth-a_-smith.

"Episcopal Diocese of New York Church Records, 1767–1970," digital image s.v. "Guy Beaumont Smith." *Ancestry.com*.

Family Bible of Antoinette Martignoni, Great-Granddaughter of James McCune Smith, n.d.

Fifteenth Annual Register of the FACNY, 1863–1864. New York: FACNY, 1863.

"Florida, Wills and Probate Records, 1810–1974," digital image s.v. "Henry Wickham Hore." *Ancestry.com*.

Fourteenth Annual Register of the FACNY, 1862–1863. New York: FACNY, 1862.

Fourth Annual Report of the ABCO. New York: ABCO, 1840.

Frothingham, Octavius B. *Gerrit Smith: A Biography*. New York: G. P. Putnam's Sons, 1878.

Furman, Guido. "Obituary of James McCune Smith." *The Medical Register of the City of New York for the Year Commencing Jun. 1, 1866*, 1866, 201–4.

Grimké, Charlotte L. *The Journals of Charlotte Forten Grimké*. Edited by Brenda E. Stevenson. New York/Oxford: Oxford University Press, 1988.

"Guy B. Smith." *TBDE*. Mar. 15, 1935.

Hobbs, Allyson Vanessa. *A Chosen Exile: A History of Racial Passing in American Life*. Cambridge: Harvard University Press, 2014

Find a Grave. "Guy B Smith (1861–1935)." Accessed Jan. 10, 2019. https://www.findagrave.com/memorial/114085944/guy-b-smith.

"Held for Wrong Registry." *TBDE*. Nov. 5, 1918.

"Henry Wickham Hore." *TBDE*. Mar. 30, 1914.

Holbrook, A. Stephen. *Holbrook's Newark City and Business Directory Official for the Year Ending Apr. 1, 1875*. Newark: A. Stephen Holbrook, 1874.

———. *Holbrook's Newark City . . . Apr. 1, 1876*. Newark: A. Stephen Holbrook, 1875.

———. *Holbrook's Newark City . . . Apr. 1, 1881*. Newark: A. Stephen Holbrook, 1880.

Holbrook, A.M. *Holbrook's Newark . . . May 1, 1887*. Newark: The Holbrook Printing Co., 1886.

———. *Holbrook's Newark . . . May 1, 1889*. Newark: The Holbrook Printing Co., 1888.

———. *Holbrook's Newark . . . May 1, 1895*. Newark: The Holbrook Printing Co., 1894.

Holbrook's Newark City . . . May 1, 1902. Newark: Holbrook Newark Directory Co., 1901.

Howard, E E. "Progress Among the Freedmen." *The Christian Recorder*. Nov. 25, 1865.

"Interment Record for Smith Family Plot at Cypress Hills Cemetery," n.d. (from Guy B. Smith descendant Greta Blau)

Find a Grave. "James Ward Smith (1845–1917)." Accessed Jan. 10, 2019. https://www.findagrave.com/memorial/35915727/james-ward-smith.

Janssen, Frederick William. *History of American Amateur Athletics*. NY: C.R. Bourne, 1885.

Lain, George T. *Brooklyn City Directory for the Year Ending May 1, 1868*. Brooklyn: J. Lain & Co., 1867.

———. *Brooklyn City Directory . . . May 1, 1871*. Brooklyn: Lain & Co., 1870.

———. *Brooklyn City Directory . . . May 1, 1878*. Brooklyn: Lain & Co., 1877.

———. *Brooklyn City Directory . . . May 1, 1881*. Brooklyn: Lain & Co., 1880.

———. *Brooklyn City Directory . . . May 1, 1889*. Brooklyn: Lain & Co., 1888.

Lain, George T., and Charles J. Healy. *Lain & Healy's Brooklyn Directory for the Year Ending May 1, 1897*. Brooklyn: Lain & Healy, 1896.

———. *Lain & Healy's Brooklyn Directory . . . May 1, 1900*. Brooklyn: Lain & Healy, 1899.

———. *Lain's Brooklyn Directory . . . May 1, 1895*. Brooklyn: Lain & Healy, 1894.

"Legal Notices: County Court, Kings County." *TBDE*. Aug. 16, 1877.

"Letter from Cousin Louise to Rebecca M. Downing," undated. George T. Downing Papers. Moorland-Spingarn Research Center, Howard University.

Longworth, Thomas. *Longworth's American Almanac, New-York Register, and City Directory*. New York: Thomas Longworth, 1839.

———. *Longworth's . . . City Directory*. New York: Thomas Longworth, 1840.

———. *Longworth's . . . City Directory*. New York: Thomas Longworth, 1843.

Find a Grave. "Maude Mary Smith (1856–1931)." Accessed Jan. 10, 2019. https://www.findagrave.com/memorial/167432432/maude-mary-smith.

McCune Smith, James. "African Colonisation—The Other Side." *National Anti-Slavery Standard*. Aug. 28, 1851.

———. "John Murray (of Glasgow)." In *Autographs for Freedom*, 1:62–67. Boston: John P. Jewett and Co., 1853.

———. Letter to the editor. *FDP*. Jan. 21, 1859.

———. Letter to the editor. *FDP*. Apr. 16, 1858.

———. Letter to the editor. *FDP*. Apr. 29, 1859.

———. Letter to the editor. *FDP*. Oct. 5, 1855.

———. *The Works of James McCune Smith: Black Intellectual and Abolitionist*. Edited by John Stauffer. Oxford: Oxford University Press, 2006

McCune Smith, James, Theodore S. Wright, and Charles B. Ray. *An Address to the Three Thousand Colored Citizens of New-York....* Gerrit Smith, 1846.

"Medical Consultations." *The Colored American*. Nov. 11, 1837.

"Memories Are Revived of Williamsburg AC" *TBDE*. Feb. 17, 1908.

Merit Roll of the FACNY, First Academic Term. New York: FACNY, 1862.

"Mrs. A.M. Smith Dies." *The Brooklyn Citizen*. Oct. 29, 1913.

Negro Population, 1790–1915. Washington, DC: United States Department of Commerce, Bureau of the Census, 1918.

"NJ, Marriage Records, 1670–1965," s.v. "Chloe Luchera Day." *Ancestry.com*.

"NYC, Public School Teacher Retirement List, 1895–1915," s.v. "Maud M. Smith." *Ancestry.com*.

New York City Telephone Directory: Brooklyn, Queens, Staten Island: May 5, 1926. New York: New York Telephone Co., 1926.

NYC Telephone Directory . . . Summer 1927. New York: New York Telephone Co., 1927.

NYC Telephone Directory . . . Summer 1928. New York: New York Telephone Co., 1928.

NYC Telephone Directory . . . Oct. 3, 1924. New York: New York Telephone Co., 1924.

NYC Telephone Directory . . . Oct. 7, 1925. New York: New York Telephone Co., 1925.

NYC Telephone Directory . . . May 15, 1920. New York: New York Telephone Co., 1920.

NYC Telephone Directory . . . Oct. 11, 1917. New York: New York Telephone Co., 1917.

NYC Telephone Directory . . . Oct. 14, 1915. New York: New York Telephone Co., 1915.

"NY Land Records, 1630–1975," digital image s.v. "Grantors/Grantees - Smith, James M.C./Malvina, His Wife." *FamilySearch.org*.

"NY Land Records, 1630–1975" digital image s.v. "Index Essex County Deeds, Grantees: Smith, James McCune." *FamilySearch.org*.

"NY, NYC Marriage Records, 1829–1940," s.v. "Marie Munn Baker." *FamilySearch.org*.

"NY, NY, Index to Death Certificates, 1862–1948: Brooklyn: 1931," s.v. "Maude Mary Smith." *Ancestry.com*.

"NY, NY, Index to Death Certificates, 1862–1948," s.v. "Melvina Smith." *Ancestry.com*.

"NY Probate Records, 1629–1971 - KC - Wills," digital image s.v. "James McCune Smith." *FamilySearch.org*.

"NY, Wills and Probate Records, 1659–1999," digital image s.v. "Eliza Barnett" (petition of Edmund W. Barnett), *Ancestry.com*.

"NY, Wills and Probate Records, 1659–1999," digital image s.v. "James P. Barnett" (probate date Jun. 2, 1883). *Ancestry.com*.

Ninth Annual Report of the GA, New York, for the Year 1857. New York: GA, 1858.

"North America, Family Histories, 1500–2000," digital image s.v. "Mrs. Chloe L. Day Smith" (Lineage Book, National Society of the Daughters of the American Revolution). *Ancestry.com*.

"Notice of Sale." *TSU*. Dec. 17, 1919.

"Obituary: Mrs. Annie Lenore Smith." *Times Union*. Mar. 31, 1915.

"Old Timers' Reunion Dinner." *The Chat*. Apr. 6, 1918.

"Old Williamsburg AC Holds Reunion Dinner." *The Brooklyn Citizen*. Mar. 8, 1926.

"Old-Time Athletes' Reunion." *The Chat*. Feb. 26, 1916.

"Park Theater." *TBDE*. Dec. 2, 1892.

"Personal: Smith." *Times Union*. Sep. 13, 1879.

Peterson, Carla L. *Black Gotham: A Family History of African Americans in Nineteenth-Century New York City*. New Haven: Yale University Press, 2011.

"Queens County Teachers' Institute." *TBDE* Apr. 25, 1889.

"Real Estate Transfers." *TBDE*. Jun. 2, 1873.

"Rites Tomorrow for Mrs. E. A. Smith." *TBDE*. Oct. 28, 1937.

Second Annual Report of the GA, New York . . . 1850. New York: William C. Bryant & Co., 1851.

Seventh Annual Report of the ABCO. New York: ABCO, 1843.

"Smith - Elizabeth A." *TBDE*. Oct. 28, 1937.

"Smith - John Murray Smith." *TBDE* May 11, 1922.

Smith, Gerrit. *Three Discourses on the Religion of Reason*. New York: Ross & Tousey, 1859.

Sutton, William H. "News of the Fraternal Societies." *TBDE*. Dec. 30, 1899.

Svenson, Sally E. *Blacks in the Adirondacks*. Syracuse: Syracuse University Press, 2017.

Tenth Annual Report of the ABCO. New York: ABCO, 1846.

"The Managers of the Colored Orphan Asylum..." *NY Journal of Commerce.* Mar. 23, 1841.

"The Negroes of New York." *The Liberator.* Aug. 25, 1865.

"The People of the State of New York." *TBDE.* Nov. 20, 1900.

"The Sixth Anniversary of the Colored Orphan Asylum." *The Evening Post.* Dec. 12, 1842.

"The Visitation's Very Excellent Theatre Party." *Times Union.* Oct. 25, 1927.

Thirteenth Annual Register of the FACNY, 1861–1862. New York: FACNY, 1861.

Tompkins, Fanny. "Report of the North Star Fair in New York." *The North Star.* Jun. 20, 1850.

Twelfth Annual Register of the FACNY, 1860–1861. New York: FACNY, 1862.

Twelfth Annual Report on the Operations and Condition of the Free Academy, by the Board of Education of the City of New York, July, 1860. New York: FACNY, 1860.

Twenty-Fourth Annual Report of the ABCO. New York: ABCO, 1861.

Twenty-Ninth Annual Report of the ABCO. New York: ABCO, 1865.

Twenty-Seventh Annual Report of the ABCO. New York: ABCO, 1864.

Twenty-Sixth Annual Report of the ABCO. New York: ABCO, 1863.

Twenty-Third Annual Report of the ABCO. New York: ABCO, 1860.

Upington, George. *Brooklyn General Directory for the Year Ending May 1, 1902.* Brooklyn: George Upington, 1901.

———. *Upington's General Directory . . . 1908.* Brooklyn: George Upington, 1908.

"Verdict for $2,550." *The Brooklyn Citizen.* Feb. 19, 1909.

"Veteran Athletes Hold Big Reunion Dinner." *TBDE.* Mar. 18, 1912.

"WAC Reunion." *Times Union.* Jan. 23, 1899.

"We Learn with Sincere Regret..." *FDP.* Jun. 10, 1853.

Wilson, Henry. *Wilson's Business Directory of New York City.* New York: John F. Trow, 1856.

Wilson, William J. Letter to the editor. *FDP.* Jan. 26, 1855.

ACKNOWLEDGEMENTS

My thanks to PhD supervisors Dr. David Silkenat and Prof. Celeste-Marie Bernier, for their invaluable guidance and advice. My thanks also to Greta Blau, for providing me with family documents pertaining to her ancestor Dr. James McCune Smith and his descendants, and giving me special access to his family tree at Ancestry.com.

Amy M. Cools is a PhD candidate in history at the University of Edinburgh. Her research focuses on the life and work of Dr. James McCune Smith, Frederick Douglass, and the history of civil rights movements, especially in the antebellum United States and Britain. She is a member of the African American Genealogical and Historical Society, British American Nineteenth Century Historians, Scottish Association for the Study of America, British Association for American Studies, and American Historical Association.

AAHGS 2021 CHAPTERS

ARKANSAS
Arkansas Chapter
Margaret Moss, President
P.O. Box 4294
Little Rock, AR 72214
arkansas@aahgs.org
www.rootsweb.com/~araahgs

CALIFORNIA
Central California Chapter
Denise Lancaster-Young, President
P.O. Box 9161 Fresno, CA 93790
aahgscc.googlepages.com
centralcali@aahgs.org

DELAWARE
Delaware Chapter
Rosalyn Green, President
P.O. Box 7205
Wilmington, DE 19803
Delaware@aahgs.org

FLORIDA
Central Florida Chapter
Alberta L. Gibbs, President
P.O. Box 681010
Orlando, FL 32802-1347
centralflorida@aahgs.org

East Central Florida Chapter
Katherine McCladdie, President
741 Ellen Street
Dayton Beach, Fl 32114
ecflorida@aahgs.org

Tampa Florida Chapter
Andria Wimberly, President
27418 Sugar Loaf Dr.
Wesley Chapel, FL 33544
tampa@aahgs.org

GEORGIA
Metro Atlanta Chapter
Tammy Ozier, President
P.O. Box 54131
Atlanta, GA 30308-9998
www.aahgsatl.org
aahgsatlanta@gmail.com

ILLINOIS
Little Egypt Chapter
Lori Crenshaw Bryant, President
P.O. Box 974
Carbondale, IL 62903-0974
hisdet911@gmail.com
littleegypt@aahgs.org

Northern Illinois Southern Wisconsin Chapter (NISW)
Carla Robinson, President
P.O. Box 1732
Rockford, IL 61110-1732
citutor2002_4u@yahoo.com
aahgsnisw.org
info@aahgsnisw.org

Patricia Liddell Researchers Chapter
Carrie McMorris, President
P.O. Box 438652
Chicago, IL 60643
patricialiddell@aahgs.org

KANSAS
Kansas Chapter
Sherri Camp, President
2601 SW Westport Dr.
Topeka, KS 66614
kansas@aahgs.org

LOUISIANA
Louisiana Chapter
Ja'el Gordon, President
PO Box 870972
New Orleans, LA 70187
Louisiana@aahgs.org

MARYLAND
Agnes Kane Callum Chapter
Roland N. Mills, President
P.O. Box 9366
Baltimore, MD 21228
baltimore@aahgs.org
https://baltimoreaahgs.org

Central Maryland Chapter
LaJoy Mosby, President
PO Box 6294
Columbia, MD 21045-9998
www.aahgscmc.org
centralmd@aahgs.org

Montgomery County, Maryland Chapter
Chiquita C. Sorrels, President
13610 Valley Drive
Rockville, MD 20850
AAHGSMCMC@gmail.com
www.aahgsmocomd.org
www.facebook.com/aahgsmocomd

Prince George's County Chapter
Jane T. Thomas, President
P.O. Box 44252
Ft. Washington, MD 20744-4252
aahgspgcm@yahoo.com
https://pgcm-aahgs.org

MASSACHUSETTS
New England Chapter
Judith Allen-Shaw, President
Five Old Planters Road
Beverly, MA 01915
newengland@aahgs.org
www.aahgs-ne.org

MINNESOTA
Minnesota Chapter
Callie Flournoy-Riser, President
P.O. Box 6289
Minneapolis, MN 55406
minnesota@aahgs.org
https://www.facebook.com/AAHGS.MTC

NEW JERSEY
New Jersey Chapter
Janice Gilyard, President
P.O. Box 5343
Somerset, NJ 08875
www.aahgsnj.org
aahgs.njchapter@gmail.com

NEW YORK
Greater New York Chapter
Sharon Wilkins, President
P.O. Box 1050
New York, NY 10116
www.aahgs-newyork.org

Richard B. Dickenson Staten Island Chapter
Debbie-Ann Paige, Robin C. Semple, Co-Presidents
456 Davis Avenue
Staten Island, NY 10310
statenisland@aahgs.org
www.sinyaahgs.blogspot.com

NORTH CAROLINA
Charlotte
Renee Jones, President
P. O Box 217283
Charlotte, NC 28390
aahgscharlotte@org

NC/Piedmont Triad Chapter
Lamar E. DeLoatch, President
P.O. Box 36254
Greensboro, NC 27416
www.ncaahgs.org

NC Sandhills Chapter
Desi L. Campbell, President
3007 Huntly Drive
Spring Lake, NC 27390
sandhills@aahgs.org

NC Triangle Chapter
Wanda Cox-Bailey, President
P.O. Box 14243
Raleigh, NC 27620
nctriangle@aahgs.org

PENNSYLVANIA
Philadelphia Family Quest Society Chapter
Allen Torrance, President
P.O. Box 34620
Philadelphia, PA 19101
familyquest@aahgs.org

Pittsburgh Chapter
Marlene Garrett Bransom, President
P.O. Box 99893
Pittsburgh, PA 15233-4893
www.aahgspgh.org
Pittsburgh@aahgs.org

TENNESSEE
East Tennessee Chapter
Shedenna A. Dockery, President
412 Ann Circle
Newport, Tennessee 37821
easttn@aahgs.org

Memphis Mid-South Chapter
Teresa Mays, President
P. O. Box 771731
Memphis, TN 38177
aahgsmemphis.org
memphis@aahgs.org
https://www.facebook.com

Nashville Chapter
Taneya Koonce, President
P.O. Box 40281
Nashville, TN 37204
www.aahgsnashville.org
nashville@aahgs.org

TEXAS
Willie Lee Gay- H-Town Chapter
Debra Blacklock Sloan, President
10418 Kelburn Drive
Houston, Texas 77016
htown@aahgs.org

UTAH
Utah Chapter
Robert Burch, President
P.O. Box 17914
Salt Lake City, UT 84117
utah@aahgs.org
www.aahgsutah.org

VIRGINIA
Burke, Brown and Steppe Chapter
April Burns, President
P.O. Box 7492
Charlottesville, VA 22906
bbsvachapter@gmail.com

Danville Chapter
Karice Luck
2132 Robin Hood Drive
Danville, VA 24540
434 441-1769
danville@aahgs.org

Greater Richmond Chapter
Larry Clark, President
P.O. Box 27833
Richmond, VA 23261
aahgsrichmond@gmail.com
www.aahgsrichmondva.com

Hampton Roads Chapter
Stephanie Thomas, President
P.O. Box 2448
Newport News, VA 23609-2448
hamptonroads@aalhgs.org

WASHINGTON, DC
James Dent Walker Chapter
Linda Crichlow White, President
P.O. Box 60632
Washington, D.C. 20039
jamesdentwalker@aahgs.org

Afro-American Historical and Genealogical Society, Inc.
P. O. Box 73067, Washington, DC 20056-3067
www.aahgs.org
National Membership Application (This application may be duplicated)

Please print or type **all** information. Missing information and/or an incomplete application causes a delay in the processing of your membership. The AAHGS membership is on a calendar year. The annual membership dues expire on December 31st. Membership is only granted after all fees are paid.

Check the AAHGS Membership categories for which you are submitting fees. You have the option of paying for multiple years. See bottom of application for payment options.
- ☐ Individual $35/year   ☐ Family $40/year   ☐ Organization $45/year
- ☐ Life Membership (individuals only) $1,000 (may be paid in three installments within a 3-year period) *

Amount enclosed _____ for membership year _____; Membership is calendar year January 1 to December

☐ New member[1]   ☐ Renewal[2]   include **Membership #:** _____   **Date:** _____

Print or type all information clearly. (Do not leave blank.)

_____
   First Name   MI   Last Name

Family membership only, full name of one family member: _____
Street Address: _____
City: _____   State: _____   Zip Code: _____
Telephone: _____   Email: _____

☐ Check here if this is a new address

Please read and complete the information below:
AAHGS Chapter to which you pay dues, if applicable. _____
Yes ☐   No ☐   Interested in joining a chapter
Yes ☐   No ☐   Interested in being contacted for a special project.
Yes ☐   No ☐   AAHGS has my permission to release my contact information for AAHGS approved initiatives.
Yes ☐   No ☐   I can accept an electronic version of the AAHGS Newsletter and AAHGS Journal [3]

Indicate Your Payment Method: (There is a $35.00 fee for all returned checks.)

❏ Check/Money Order payable to **AAHGS**   **NO CASH PLEASE**

❏ Credit Card: American Express, Discover, Master Card or Visa

_____   _____
Credit Card Number   Expiration Date (mm/yyyy)

Name as written on credit card: _____   CSV _____

Mail to: AAHGS-Membership; P.O. Box 73067; Washington, DC 20056-3067
(Applications and checks mailed to any other address incur significant delays in processing)

[1] First time *member applications received before September 1 will receive the next scheduled AAHGS Newsletters and all back issues for the current calendar year. First time member applications received after September 1, are granted membership through December 31 of the next calendar year and will begin receiving the AAHGS' newsletters with the next scheduled mailing of the newsletter.*
[2] Renewal *applications received after January 31st will begin receiving the AAHGS Newsletters starting with the next scheduled mailing.*
*Life Membership payments must be completed within three years of the initial payment.
[3] Hard copy of AAHGS NEWS: ($6.00) - HARD COPY OF AAHGS JOURNAL: ($35.00)

Allow **10-14 days** for processing after receipt of your application by Membership Services

Do Not Remove. For office use only: ID#: _____   N ____ R ____ REN ____
DMR: _____   DDE: _____   DME: _____
Notes:

Index

African American, 2, 5, 6, 7, 9, 10, 11, 13, 14, 16, 17, 18, 19, 20, 21, 22, 24, 25, 26, 29, 31, 33, 34, 35, 36, 37, 38, 40, 41, 37, 55, 57, 58, 59, 63, 65, 68, 69, 74, 76, 92, 68
African Methodist Episcopal, 46, 49, 50, 53
Alexander, 6, 27, 35, 36
Allen, 41, 46, 66, 71, 75, 92
Andrews, 32, 65, 71, 73, 87, 91
Angola, 28, 29, 37
Anthony, 10, 11, 12, 13, 14, 18, 22, 35, 38, 40, 43
Auld, 41, 43, 44, 45, 46, 47, 48, 49, 50, 53, 54
Bailey, 41, 42, 54, 92
Baker, 73, 82, 90
Baptist, 9, 16
Barbados, 12, 39
Barnett, 6, 7, 57, 59, 60, 68, 77, 78, 79, 80, 81, 82, 83, 84, 85, 86, 87, 88, 89, 90, 91, 92, 93, 63, 64, 70, 71, 73, 74, 75, 76, 77, 78, 81, 82, 84, 85, 90
Beaumont, 59, 60, 77, 78, 85, 92, 64, 75, 77, 84, 87
Bell, 36, 63, 64, 65, 66, 67, 71, 72, 73
Bennett, 10, 11, 12, 13, 39
Biggs, 36
Bowser, 6, 7, 9, 10, 11, 12, 13, 14, 15, 17, 18, 19, 20, 21, 22, 24, 25, 35, 36, 38, 39, 40, 41, 42
Case, 25, 34, 41, 69, 76, 87, 94
Civil War, 10, 11, 25, 34, 38, 39, 68, 69, 74, 87, 92
Clifford, 13
Coker, 46, 48
Cumbo, 6, 7, 27, 28, 29, 30, 31, 32, 33, 34, 35, 36, 38
Davis, 27, 29, 30, 31, 33, 34, 92
Delany, 72, 74, 66, 79, 86
Donegan, 75
Downing, 72, 81, 87, 88
Driggers, 35, 38
Foster, 85
Frederick Douglass, 6, 7, 41, 42, 52, 54, 55, 62, 68, 74, 75, 63, 64, 66, 77, 79, 84
Gordon, 25, 34, 41, 38, 92
Great Britain, 12
Gregory, 34, 41, 42
Grice, 46
Grimké, 70, 80, 87
Guiana, 50
Hamilton, 22, 61, 65, 69, 72, 74
Hollie, 6, 41
Hoosier, 46
Hore, 74, 75, 83, 87
Howe, 24
Hunt, 25, 34, 35, 38, 41, 42
Irish, 27, 45, 46, 68
Jay, 63, 70, 76, 81
Johnson, 50
Joubert, 49
Kearns, 6, 27, 35, 36
Kemp, 2, 29, 30, 31
Kingdom of Ndongo, 27, 28, 29, 31, 36
Lawson, 50
Lewis, 50, 59, 77, 78, 86, 90
Liberia, 22
Lively, 49
Lloyd, 41, 42, 44, 45
Locks, 50, 51, 53, 55
Lowery, 36
Lumbee, 27
Lutheran, 74
Lyons, 62, 67, 69, 71, 75
Martignoni, 64, 75, 79, 87
Maryland, 7, 10, 11, 13, 15, 22, 39, 41, 42, 43, 45, 46, 51, 55, 56, 92
McCune, 6, 7, 57, 58, 59, 61, 62, 63, 64, 65, 66, 67, 68, 69, 70, 71, 72, 73, 74, 75, 77, 80, 81, 85, 86, 87, 90, 94, 63, 64, 65, 66, 67, 68, 69, 70, 71, 72, 74, 75, 76, 77, 78, 79, 80, 83, 84, 85, 86, 87, 89, 90, 91
Melungeon, 27
Methodist, 46, 48, 49, 51, 52, 55, 56, 66, 71, 75, 76
Mitchell, 53
Murray, 19, 40, 42, 51, 60, 64, 70, 74, 75, 83, 89, 90
New York, 39, 40, 37, 52, 55, 57, 59, 61, 62, 63, 64, 65, 66, 68, 69, 70, 71, 72, 73, 74, 75, 76, 77, 78, 79, 80, 81, 83, 84, 85, 86, 87, 88, 89, 90, 91, 92, 93, 94, 63, 65, 66, 67, 68, 69, 70, 71, 72, 76, 79, 80, 82, 84, 86, 87, 88, 89, 90, 91, 92
North Carolina, 9, 10, 11, 14, 18, 22, 23, 24, 25, 26, 27, 33, 36, 37, 39, 40, 36, 68, 71, 76
Oblate Sisters of Providence, 49
Parker, 59, 69, 78, 79, 80, 81, 82, 84, 85, 86, 87, 89, 91, 71, 72, 73, 78
Patterson, 25, 41
Peck, 50
Pennington, 52
Pennsylvania, 13
Pierce, 2, 30
Piersey, 34, 35
Portuguese, 27, 28, 30
Quakers, 46
Revolutionary War, 21, 38, 72
Richards, 36
Riley, 75
Rohrer, 74
Rolles, 51
Roman Catholic, 49, 74, 76
Roosevelt, 80, 87, 88
Sabbath School, 49
Sanderlin, 25, 41
Shroy, 74
Smith, 6, 7, 41, 32, 57, 58, 59, 60, 61, 62, 63, 64, 65, 66, 67, 68, 69, 70, 71, 72, 73, 74, 75, 76, 77, 78, 80, 81, 82, 85, 86, 87, 88, 89, 90, 93, 94, 63, 64, 65, 66, 67, 68, 69, 70, 71, 72, 73, 74, 75, 76, 77, 78, 79, 80, 81, 82, 83, 84, 85, 86, 87, 88, 89, 90, 91
South Carolina, 10, 35, 40, 59, 61, 65, 71, 76
Spaulding, 36
Spelman, 25, 41
Thomas, 2, 25, 35, 41, 42, 31, 32, 46, 53, 55, 68, 70, 71, 72, 74, 75, 86, 93, 78, 88, 92, 93
Tyson, 49
Virginia, 9, 10, 11, 12, 13, 14, 15, 17, 18, 19, 21, 22, 23, 24, 25, 26, 29, 30, 34, 36, 39, 40, 42, 27, 29, 30, 31, 32, 33, 35, 36, 37, 38
Wallis, 40
Ward, 60, 69, 82, 86, 88, 90, 63, 66, 67, 69, 71, 72, 73, 78, 81, 82, 85, 88
Waters, 50
Watkins, 46, 49
Watkins Academy, 49
Weaver, 65, 66, 71, 75, 76
Wells, 49, 50, 68, 76
West Indies, 77
White, 9, 10, 13, 15, 18, 19, 23, 26, 27, 28, 29, 31, 33, 34, 35, 36, 37, 27, 31, 81, 67, 71, 93
Wilson, 25, 41, 86, 89, 94, 80, 81, 91
Woods, 23, 37, 40, 78, 79, 82, 83

www.ingramcontent.com/pod-product-compliance
Lightning Source LLC
Chambersburg PA
CBHW041519220426

43667CB00002B/41